Good and Wealthy

Good and Wealthy

Prosperous Women and Men Who Led Saintly Lives

Ronald Quillo

RESOURCE *Publications* · Eugene, Oregon

GOOD AND WEALTHY
Prosperous Women and Men Who Led Saintly Lives

Copyright © 2025 Ronald Quillo. All rights reserved. Except for brief quotations in critical publications or reviews, no part of this book may be reproduced in any manner without prior written permission from the publisher. Write: Permissions, Wipf and Stock Publishers, 199 W. 8th Ave., Suite 3, Eugene, OR 97401.

Resource Publications
An Imprint of Wipf and Stock Publishers
199 W. 8th Ave., Suite 3
Eugene, OR 97401

www.wipfandstock.com

PAPERBACK ISBN: 979-8-3852-3478-3
HARDCOVER ISBN: 979-8-3852-3479-0
EBOOK ISBN: 979-8-3852-3480-6

Scripture quotations are taken from the *New Revised Standard Version Updated Edition*. Copyright © 2021 National Council of Churches of Christ in the United States of America. Used by permission. All rights reserved worldwide.

For My Family,
All of Whom
Have Enriched My Life
Beyond Measure

Contents

Preface: The Unlikely Virtuous xi
    Exceptions Proving the Rule xi
    Exceptional Prosperity xi
    Pointing the Way? xii

Introduction: Wealth and Spirituality—The Challenge of Luxury and Privilege xiii
    Heralding Peril xiii
    Virtue in the Midst of Splendor xiv
    Respecting Reports of Virtue xv
    Historical Models xvi

Chapter 1: Notable Living—Remarkable Exemplars of Goodness 1
    Saint Guntram—A Cad Turned Good 1
    Saint Adelaide—A Lady Adorable and Tough 2
    Saint Homobonus—A Philanthropic Businessman 5
    Saint Elzéar of Sabran and Blessed Delphine of Glandèves—A Marriage of Uncommon Devotion 7
    Saint Ferdinand III—A Royal Champion and Hero Bigger than Life 9
    Saint Margaret of Scotland—A Ravishing Royal Beauty 12
    Saint Louis IX—An Accomplished Ruler with an Assertive Mother 14
    Venerable Pierre Toussaint—Freely a Slave 15
    Blessed Frédéric Ozanam—A Renowned Scholar with a Tender Heart 19
    Blessed Victoire Rasoamanarivo—A Royal Champion of the Oppressed 22
    Saints Louis and Marie-Azélie Martin—An Industrious and Dedicated Couple 25
    Saint Gianna Beretta Molla—Generosity Beyond Measure 27

Contents

Blesseds Luigi and Maria Beltrame Quattrocchi—An Extraordinary Couple Extraordinarily in Love 29

Chapter 2: Contours of Possession—Pleasures of Wealth 32
   Saint Guntram—Bathed in Opulence 32
   Saint Adelaide—Royal Retinue and Real Estate 33
   Saint Homobonus—Quite Comfortably Situated 34
   Saint Elzéar of Sabran and Blessed Delphine of Glandèves—The Young Picture-Perfect Couple Awash in Splendor 35
   Saint Ferdinand III—Riches Beyond Compare 37
   Saint Margaret of Scotland—A Lady of Refined Tastes 39
   Saint Louis IX—The Epitome of Royal Luxury 41
   Venerable Pierre Toussaint—Enriched in Many Ways 42
   Blessed Frédéric Ozanam—A Keen Sense of the Pleasurable 44
   Blessed Victoire Rasoamanarivo—Cultured Taste and Proper Refinement 46
   Saints Louis and Marie-Azélie Martin—A Prosperous, Enterprising Couple 47
   Saint Gianna Beretta Molla—Enjoying Familial Delights 49
   Blesseds Luigi and Maria Beltrame Quattrocchi—Rich in Family Life 50

Chapter 3: Making the Most of Things—Tenets and Tactics 53
   Saint Guntram—Anger Tamed and Refined 53
   Saint Adelaide—Shrewd Diplomat and Productive Manager 54
   Saint Homobonus—Energetic and Crafty 56
   Saint Elzéar of Sabran and Blessed Delphine of Glandèves—Adroit Managers 57
   Saint Ferdinand III—An Exemplary Commander Who Prized Subsidiarity 59
   Saint Margaret of Scotland—A Queen with Administrative Sense 63
   Saint Louis IX—A Modest King with a Heart of Gold 65
   Venerable Pierre Toussaint—Master of His Trade, Admired Citizen 69
   Blessed Frédéric Ozanam—Practical Organizer and Inspiring Theorist 72
   Blessed Victoire Rasoamanarivo—A Kindly Executive 75
   Saints Louis and Marie-Azélie Martin—Productive and Admired Partners 76
   Saint Gianna Beretta Molla—Intent on Service 78

Contents

Blesseds Luigi and Maria Beltrame Quattrocchi—Eminently Refined and Eminently Engaged 79

Chapter 4: Living Fully—Godly Energy 83
Saint Guntram—A Schmoozing, Kindly Public Servant 83
Saint Adelaide—Modestly Magnanimous 85
Saint Homobonus—Outstanding Productivity and Passionate Concern 87
Saint Elzéar of Sabran and Blessed Delphine of Glandèves—Passionate Virgins 90
Saint Ferdinand III—Lifelong Devotion 93
Saint Margaret of Scotland—Infectious Spirituality 98
Saint Louis IX—Lover of Virtue 102
Venerable Pierre Toussaint—Propagator of Good Cheer 106
Blessed Frédéric Ozanam—A Countercultural Advocate for Justice 109
Blessed Victoire Rasoamanarivo—A Mightily Influential Convert 112
Saints Louis and Marie-Azélie Martin—Spiritually Minded Parents 114
St. Gianna Beretta Molla—A Physician in Spiritual Residency 117
Blesseds Luigi and Maria Beltrame Quattrocchi—Profound and Uncommonly Fruitful Faith 119

Conclusion: Illustrious Prosperity—Exemplary Richness 126
The Treacherous Allure of Wealth 126
Wealth as Treacherous but Surmountable 126
Wealth as a Blessing 128
The Ambiguity of Riches 129
Riches and Responsibility 130
Above and Beyond 136

Bibliography 139

Preface: The Unlikely Virtuous

EXCEPTIONS PROVING THE RULE

THE VAST MAJORITY OF those traditionally or officially called saints, blessed, or venerable have been poor, either by life circumstances or by choice—namely, by historical conditioning or by a formal vow of poverty. Their simplicity is imposing and edifying. Their astoundingly large number supports biblical observations regarding the desirability of poverty for spiritual accomplishment or advancement. But there are exceptional cases, which are in their unique ways imposing and edifying. This book is about extraordinary women and men who represent a small minority among the sainted, blessed, or venerated—namely, the few who were quite wealthy, some even splendorously, or whose prosperity was at least notable and in large measure agreeable. They lived and died well off materially but nonetheless attained what has been observed as heights of sanctity. They did not in the end give all their fortunes away, as so many illustrious among the saintly have done, nor were they murdered or martyred because of their virtue, as hundreds of admirable personalities sadly have been—whether or not they were among the prosperous. They did not become clerics or enter institutional religious communities, as have legions of those called holy.

EXCEPTIONAL PROSPERITY

The lay heroes of this book are some impressively virtuous luminaries who remained famously rich or steadfastly prosperous throughout their lives. They were affluent or well-situated people who lived during the sixth through the twentieth centuries, who were recognized and admired

Preface: The Unlikely Virtuous

during the own lifetimes for extraordinary virtue and who continued to evoke devotion after their deaths. The charitable influence of these once earthly personalities—later claimed heavenly—was, to many, stunningly and miraculously evident. Centuries ago holiness such as theirs was thus popularly acclaimed and each was given a title such as *saint*. Somewhat later, around the thirteenth century, on the basis of witnesses and evidence carefully reviewed, such honored individuals began to be variously canonized—institutionally or officially proclaimed *venerable*, *blessed*, or *saint*—typically by papal decree. They were historical models, precedents of some praiseworthy individuals who even today, noticeably or inconspicuously, proceed admirably by their noble principles and genial beneficence.

POINTING THE WAY?

In our times such generous persons are philanthropists who are spiritually or religiously motivated. They are the fortunate who enjoy the good things of life, profess a faith, and generously attend to many in need. With such persons in mind, and with hope of inspiring their growth in numbers, we may look to the lives of some of the saintly prosperous.

Introduction: Wealth and Spirituality— The Challenge of Luxury and Privilege

HERALDING PERIL

"WOE TO YOU WHO are rich..." (Luke 6:24). This cry resounds thunderously and sometimes threateningly throughout the ages, challenging those attentive to biblical teachings or guided by spiritual values. These striking words of Jesus shock, or at least give pause. They echo the prophetic warning to ancient Israel that wealth can lead—and not infrequently—to overwrought self-esteem (Ezek 28:5), greed (Mic 2:2) or oppression (Ezek 2:29). Such words challenge facile satisfaction in one's material values and possessions. And they are amplified by the warning that, "indeed, it is easier for a camel to go through the eye of a needle than for someone who is rich to enter the kingdom of God" (Luke 18:25). Hearing cautions like this, a believer could readily wonder whether anyone of means can benefit from spirituality or the practice of a religion. In such a quandary one might either despair in the midst of one's own wealth or disdain those among the very prosperous. When riches appear under such a shadow, can there be any welcoming of luxury? When riches have been depicted as dangerous or destructive, as a threat to virtuous or saintly living, the outlook on prosperity seems bleak. And not unreasonably, given the avarice of individuals or detrimental cultural influences upon them.[1] It can hardly be disputed that there have been sad examples of the rich who have been haughty, selfish, or exploitive and thus hardly notable examples of sanctity. One thinks of the infamous Nero or the fabulous Scrooge. By contrast, many women and men heralded as holy, or named saintly in the Christian tradition, have been either poor all

---

1. Ward, *Wealth and Moral Luck*, 133–70.

Introduction: Wealth and Spirituality

their lives or have eventually deigned to renounce all their wealth in order to practice virtues facilitated by impoverishment.

VIRTUE IN THE MIDST OF SPLENDOR

Yet the very Bible advocating such renunciation pays considerable attention to other personalities who are particularly provocative in a converse way—namely, who are paragons of faith and enjoy notable wealth, or even an abundance of it. Kings of Israel—like David, Solomon, and Josiah—despite all their faults, are depicted in the long view as exemplars of virtue. They live royally and reign in grand style. They govern through multiple administrators and are central to an aristocracy. Their treasure abounds and even swells while they embody wisdom and goodness. In later times Jesus approvingly tells of a nobleman who, having attained royal status, encourages his servants to make profitable investments (Luke 19:12–19). In this story there is markedly no disparagement of pursuing wealth. Jesus also praises a well-established philanthropic Roman centurion for having great faith (Luke 7:1–9). And personalities of apparently significant means—like Joanna (Luke 8:3),[2] Nicodemus (John 19:38–40), and Joseph of Arimathea (Matt 27:57–58)—revered Jesus and provided him with various measures of support. As to the Bible's approach to grandeur, Jesus is depicted there as king (e.g., John 12:13–15) and even depicts himself as a one (Matt 25:34). Clearly then it is a stretch to reduce the Bible's forceful warnings about wealth to an absolute or universally binding condemnation of riches. Sanctity in the midst of wealth, while seemingly unattainable, is indeed by divine grace quite possible (Luke 18:26–27).

The aim of the present book is to explore the lives of prosperous saintly personalities. Such women and men enjoyed great wealth yet came to be honored among Christians—and among many others of good will—as models of virtue or holiness. Their lives are exceptional, considering biblical cautions against wealth, and noting the staggering number of saintly personalities who historically were noted for their poverty. So it is understandable that, at times, the biographers of revered women and men showered with riches blush at their protagonists' abundance, or even apologize for it. In light of teachings about the dangers of wealth, these virtuous people defeated the odds. But did they really? Did they basically overcome an imposing bulwark against virtue, or did they to a greater extent draw

2. Hays, *Renouncing Everything*, 42, 73.

Introduction: Wealth and Spirituality

upon a larger wisdom, a sense of what suffuses the marrow of virtue and thus nurtures sanctity or fosters profound and satisfying spirituality? What was it about their virtue and their wealth that made them exceptional?

RESPECTING REPORTS OF VIRTUE

A close examination of such fascinating lives and marvelous exploits elicits some provocative answers, which will be considered after surveying how these saintly personalities lived and managed their wealth. But an important observation is due. The lives of revered women and men are largely based on sources prone to celebrate the virtues of their protagonists. The biographies contain varying explanations of the saintly personalities' motives and behaviors. The biographers were thus biased in their subjects' favor. Some historiographers tell us that such bias, positive or negative, affects in varying degrees all historical treatises. Such is understandable due to the writers' personal perspectives and, in the case of hagiography—stories of saints or holy people—to the authors' enthusiasm and even devotion.

Yet their very hesitance to glorify their subjects' endowment with wealth adds credulity to claims about such wealth's significance. If the biographers were forthright enough to blush at the saints' material endowments, one can reasonably suspect that they must be honest enough to provide essentially reliable accounts of the saints' virtues attained in settings of considerable and sometimes massive riches. Moreover the Catholic Church historically has been careful and even rigorous in examining witnesses to the lives of those who might be canonized.[3] Admittedly there is yet to be articulated a precise methodology for differentiating historical accuracy from reverential literary reportage in the ancient or classical sources for the lives of the saints.[4] Yet even a recent careful biographer who is skeptical of what might seem like excessive claims of a distant age regarding sanctity can admit that a "substratum of truth"[5] remains respectable. Chroniclers of old can remain essentially credible both despite and because of their intense loyalty to their subjects. And honorable portrayals of what is saintly communicate what is worthy of esteem, even if some details appear historically magnified. Such biographies, not always by historians, may contain

---

3. Vauchez, *Sainthood in the Middle Ages*, 37.
4. Kitchen, *Saints' Lives*, 8.
5. Dunlop, *Queen Margaret of Scotland*, 7.

Introduction: Wealth and Spirituality

exaggerations but not fabrications.[6] Many of the saintly personalities so depicted have a certain storybook aura that make tales of them not only historically informative and inspiring but also entertaining. They compellingly illustrate the ways by which their enjoyment of great wealth can be acceptable and praiseworthy, even in a spiritual tradition where the pursuit and enjoyment of wealth is deemed quite risky.

HISTORICAL MODELS

We may candidly and woefully observe that, historically and currently, too many persons endowed with wealth have succumbed to such pitfalls as greed, selfishness, and exploitation. But we can also kindly hope that in the chronicles of some whose wealth accompanied sanctity, an admirable number of today's affluent will find something of their own stories. With such in mind, let us proceed with some tales of the saintly prosperous. The book is organized so that saintly individuals' lives can be examined in tandem from different perspectives. Here then will ensue not a series of thoroughgoing biographies but topical snapshots rendering various facets of the subjects' lives. The snapshots or vignettes will be gathered thematically in different chapters. First appear in broad strokes a major segment of each saintly personality's life (ch. 1). Then follow surveys of the wealth that each person enjoyed (ch. 2). After a depiction of each one's professional, administrative, and/or leadership achievements (ch. 3) comes a presentation of the particular virtues characterizing each of their lives (ch. 4). The concluding segment considers why such a boding threat as wealth can nonetheless shape in praiseworthy ways the lives of the venerable, the blessed, saints, and all people of good will (ch. 5).

---

6. Wilson, *St. Margaret*, 135.

CHAPTER 1

Notable Living—Remarkable Exemplars of Goodness

The following vignettes briefly sketch the vibrant and impressive lives of admirable personalities who have dotted the remote and recent past. Be they giants of history or among those who have contributed gigantically to time's humane countenance, they exhibit traits that are captivating and sometimes astounding. By color and contour, some of their histories resemble fairy tales but without being fanciful. However dramatically, these women and men vividly illustrate how virtue amplifies the artistry of wholesome and productive living. Having considered these summary biographies, we will in later chapters examine in detail the various characteristics by which these notable figures may tellingly be called saintly and prosperous—or good and wealthy.

SAINT GUNTRAM—A CAD TURNED GOOD

Of all the personalities in this book, King Guntram might appear the least likely to have been named a saint. His early life was so offbeat, and even shameful, that it could have permanently diverted him from the virtue by which he became, though some would say barely, renowned.

He once callously cheated his brother's widow out of her extensive inheritance, his own wealth lusting for more of the same. Yet his reprehensible treatment of an in-law would limp far in the wake of other vices. Guntram was subject to fits of inordinate if not savage cruelty. In the treatment of enemies, he could resort to brutalities of torture. Glibly disregarding the sanctity of life, he maliciously ordered the executions of a few acquaintances that he disdained.[1]

Hardly scrupulous in relating with women, he first pleasured royally in concubinage, then entered two serial marriages, producing children by each of the three arrangements.[2] Courage was hardly his specialty. At even a hint of threat to his life or limb, he could go into a panic. Fear of assassination haunted him constantly, so that even in his later years he always wore extra armor and commanded a retinue of hefty bodyguards.

He was a Merovingian, a scion of the royal family that reigned over the medieval kingdom of the Franks, part of present-day France and Germany. Born in AD 532, his father King Clothar I left him an extensive portion of the kingdom, thus making him King of Burgundy in 561.[3] Despite his peculiar if not eccentric and disdainful behavior of his earlier years, as a sovereign he eventually enjoyed widespread popularity among the citizenry and largely exhibited quite reformed and honorable character traits.[4] This was a substantial turnaround, as we will see in subsequent chapters.

Guntram's early mannerisms and behavior contrast starkly with the emergent years of the others in this book. Their younger days were more commendable, and their environments, more conducive to the stature and admiration that they acquired as adults.

SAINT ADELAIDE—A LADY ADORABLE AND TOUGH

In the year 931 the Burgundian King Rudolf II welcomed into his household the newborn Adelaide (also known as Adelheid). The bleakness of the countryside in which the nation's capital was set forebode the several sorry instances that would mark her life. Still unanticipated were the many rays of light that would nonetheless illuminate her journey early on as queen and later as an empress. The little girl would know her father for only six years. His death was the first of her sorrows.

But with time came sunbeams. As a young woman of sixteen, she would be given in marriage to Prince Lothaire, son of King Hugh of Italy. Her betrothal to the youthful Lothaire had been instigated by Hugo some ten years earlier. The then six-year-old little girl and eight-year-old boy

---

1. Thierry, *Early Franks*, 17, 91.
2. Wikipedia, "Guntram I," para. 3.
3. Bennett, "Guntramnus," 432.
4. Butler, *Lives*, 1:695–96.

grew up together, playing and learning amid the trappings of the royal Italian throne at Pavia. Their eventual marriage was unusual however, not by her young age but by the fact that her mother had at the time of the betrothal married the womanizer Hugh, becoming his fourth wife and thus rendering Lothaire Adelaide's stepbrother and, by an intricate lineage, her second cousin. The church frowned upon this but sometimes tolerated local custom.

Yet the couple's marriage was not merely an arranged one of political convenience but, more importantly, one of mutual love and commitment. Lothaire was demonstrably a kind and sensitive young man who did not share his father's unscrupulous values but early on warmly regarded the beautiful Adelaide as a girl worthy of esteem and protection. She, the adorable princess, would become the wife whom he would call his sweet and beloved. Some two years after their marriage the young couple's daughter Emma was born.

Sadly the happy marriage was not to last. Through intrigues invented by Berengarius of Ivrea, a rival for the Italian throne, Lothaire became king. Though his sovereignty was only nominal—Berengarius held a tight rein on the throne—Lothaire was a dedicated king and a largely effective ruler; and Adelaide became, in these circumstances, the queen of Italy. But just three years later Lothaire died, seemingly poisoned by Berengarius, leaving Adelaide to her tears. Berengarius thereupon had himself crowned king and pledged Adelaide—not unsuspiciously—to his son and her second cousin, Adalbert, in marriage. The young widow staunchly refused to marry an ally of her deceased husband's opponent and by such a marriage threaten her own claim to the Italian throne.[5] With that, Berengarius began to physically abuse her,[6] punching and kicking her while tearing at her hair,[7] and tried to impoverish her by confiscating what he could of her fortune.[8] Finally, he had her placed in near-solitary confinement, allowing only a chaplain and a maid to assist her. The little daughter, Emma, was confided to an unknown person's care.

The walls that Adelaide faced for four months were likely those of a nearby castle. Not to lessen the drama however, an inventive priest named Father Martin helped her and the maid dig an escape tunnel under the

---

5. Golinelli, *Adelaide*, 44, 46–47, 50, 54–56, 61–62.
6. Odilo of Cluny, *Epitaph*, 130.
7. Schneider Berrenberg, *Adelheid*, 9.
8. Goullet, "Hrostvita de Gandersheim," 48.

castle wall, led them and the maid into the woods for hiding, and kept them nourished with fish caught by his own hand. Meantime they were continually pursued, in constant danger of being recaptured. When the Duke of Canossa heard of this, he raced to her rescue and gave her a home in his castle.

Meantime the future Holy Roman emperor, the German Otto I (or Otto the Great) acted effectively on his plans to take Italy as his own domain. Having heard of entreaties from Adelaide, the German sovereign, who had been widowed for five years,[9] made his way to Canossa, met her there, and was overwhelmed by her beauty, which indeed was extraordinary and renowned.[10] But his attention to her was not just emotional or aesthetic. In his eyes her famed physical attractiveness was more than matched, as he noted with careful discernment, by her likewise famed virtue. Moreover she appeared to him as woman of fortitude and competence. And she gladly welcomed his attention.[11]

The ensuing romance led to their marriage. By then she was twenty years old and twenty years younger than her new husband.[12] Celebrated in a church setting with the prayers of the clergy, the union was for Adelaide one that she devotedly accepted as a blessing, and with appropriate passion. The royal couple would eventually have three living children; their first and two later children would die at very early ages, adding more sorrowful shading to the lustrous contours of her life.

While Otto's initial plans for Italy had not immediately materialized militarily, Adelaide's popularity with the citizenry greatly facilitated his eventual subjugation of the country. From their endearment to her followed the population's allegiance to him. Sometime after the wedding, Otto was crowned emperor by the pope, and Adelaide was crowned empress. During a six-year period she lived in Rome as Otto ruled from there. The imperial family then returned to the palatial home in Germany. The people there too idolized her for her affection and endearing manner.

She well complemented the various accomplishments of her husband Otto I, standing by him and representing his policies in his absence. He was regarded as Europe's greatest emperor, second only to the notable

---

9. Gilsdorf, introduction to *Queenship*, 6; Gilsdorf, notes to *Queenship*, 187.
10. Bäumer, *Otto und Adelheid*, 13–14, 35.
11. Nash, *Empress Adelheid*, 136–39.
12. Butler, *Lives*, 4:572.

Charlemagne. With Otto's death, Adelaide became, at forty-two, a widow for the second time; and her son, Otto II, became emperor.

Though newly weighted with a widow's grief, her eminence hardly ceased. Her years during Otto II's marriage with the notorious Theaphanu, a celebrated noble of Greek lineage,[13] were quite turbulent due to the animosity of the jealous daughter-in-law. Under such pressure and the added denunciation by Otto her son, Adelaide regretfully but temporarily retired from the imperial palace to the castle of her brother Conrad, king of Burgundy. With her vibrant personality she typically brought much delight to the locals. But she returned to Otto's court after a kindly abbot, Majolus of Cluny, had negotiated a reconciliation. The son's repentance met the mother's forgiveness. The peace between them endured until his untimely death shortly thereafter. With the ascent of her young grandson, Otto III, to the throne, Theaphanu's intrigues hardly ceased, and the again beleaguered Adelaide was forced anew to withdraw from the palace. But with Theaphanu's death, Adelaide was recalled to imperial court to serve as regent,[14] a position she held for four years—much to the appreciation of her youthful and still minor grandson, the soon-to-be newly crowned emperor.[15] The situation would add to her fame.

SAINT HOMOBONUS—A PHILANTHROPIC BUSINESSMAN

In medieval Italian he was called Omobono Tucenghi. Commonly known historically as Homobonus (Latin for "the good man"), he was born in the northern Italian city of Cremona. It was the early twelfth century, about the year 1111. His father was a successful businessman who, though relatively uneducated himself, grounded Homobonus well in matters of the clothing trade and admirably instilled in him strengths of character. The apple did not fall far from the tree. Homobonus avidly assumed the family business and became familiar with its various aspects, first as a tailor and later as a vendor of clothing and soft goods, especially wool. He was a zealous businessman.

But he was not as content with his city's culture. Entrepreneurial productivity did not undermine his sense of social responsibility. As an

---

13. Golinelli, *Adelaide*, 63–64, 80–81, 84, 122, 133, 136–37.
14. Campbell, "St. Adelaide."
15. Odilo of Cluny, *Epitaph*, 133–34.

adolescent he sometimes felt like fleeing the brawls and ruckus of his fellow youths in the neighborhood. They were acting out of hand and it was only right to avoid them. Later in life he would influence his fellow citizens in more positive ways, as we will see.

He was tall and robust, with a practical athletic build that was a lifelong endowment. As a young man clearly filled with characteristic exuberant passion, he was eminently disposed toward marriage, a sentiment on which he eventually acted with vibrant commitment and with the support of his parents. Besides fondly regarding their sentiments, he was without doubt appreciative spiritually of their vowed sacramental marriage. Moreover, as a man of his medieval times, he regarded wedlock as beneficial economically; accompaniment by a faithful spouse eased his busy work life and complemented his image—not that his vows would be in any way insincere. His personal values would assuredly have inclined him toward an enduring and heartfelt love of his marital partner.

So he chose a young woman with whom he could so live, someone with whom he could find brighter and more hope-filled days. Sadly, we do not know her name. We do know however that she was a good woman, dutiful in her spirituality, and charitable. Plus she proved to be a fine administrator of the household.[16] In accord with the usage of the times, their mutual commitment would have included a church wedding, a blessing of their house, and their joyful expectation of having children. His biographers differ on the number of their offspring.

Whether the pair had no children at all, or possibly several, is inconclusive.[17] Whatever the case, Homobonus managed to enjoy considerable success in business while turning to philanthropic and civic interests by a kind of natural disposition. His wife fully supported him in his propensities, though she could become impatient as the poor came to the door at all hours with their appeals. For her a more orderly approach, especially by those who offended by their smell and grime, would have been more welcome. She loved and adored her husband, never speaking a harsh word against him and even gladdening him with her concurrence in his generosity. But the constant turmoil of the household at times seemed to her overwhelming.[18] In a context of varying interests then, the successful and

---

16. Butler, *Lives*, 4:334.
17. Ricci, "OMOBONO da Cremona," para. 5.
18. Pedretti, *Sant' Omobono*, 22, 25–26, 29–33.

prosperous businessman Homobonus would have an astounding impact on his community and on what would become the memory of him.

SAINT ELZÉAR OF SABRAN AND BLESSED DELPHINE OF GLANDÈVES—A MARRIAGE OF UNCOMMON DEVOTION

Born in 1286 to a noble and illustrious family of Provence in France, the intellectually gifted Elzéar was well educated in sunnier southern Marseilles under the tutelage of his uncle, the Abbot William of Sabran. At the age of ten, innocent Elzéar was promised in marriage to Delphine of Glandèves (also known as Delphine de Signe or de Puymichel), a sweet girl about his age, probably two years older. She was the daughter of a nobleman and his wealthy wife but sadly had become an orphan at the age of seven, financially secured by the inheritance of her father's fortune. At the urging of the Neapolitan king, who was also a Provençal nobleman, the handsome Elzéar eventually married the lovely young woman when, by the current norms, the time was appropriate.

At first she had vigorously rejected the young gentleman's proposal, which he initially made to her indirectly through a representative. Her care during her younger years had been relegated to her uncles and her education assigned to her aunt, who was an abbess. Exceptionably religious and, for six years, highly impressed by the lives of the nuns in the abbey, Delphine's terms of marriage, which she formulated after a good deal of soul searching, included the unusual stipulation that she remain a virgin. Hearing of her demand, Elzéar was for a good while—as one would expect—hesitant to agree. But after meeting her, he rather quickly grew to love her dearly. He not only regarded her beauty as intensely alluring but was fondly drawn as well to her traits of character. The question for him was whether an enthralling life with her was worth her stipulation.

After searching his soul, itself well developed in virtue, and with the encouragement of a Franciscan friar, Elzéar ultimately acceded to her wishes. Together in devoted marriage, they continued their own spiritual practices while admirably attending to both familial and social commitments. Their love for one another was in fact quite intense, and it showed in many ways. Delphine, for example, was tenderly attentive to Elzéar's moods. And his sentiments for her were pronounced—visible, for example, by his tears when praying for her when she was seriously ill.[19]

19. Butler, *Lives*, 3:661–62; Bernard, *Époux vierges*, 31, 54–56, 66–67.

So their marriage, though atypical, was widely admired in their circles. To even the careful observer, they were clearly in love and profoundly dedicated to one another; it was thus presumed that their marriage had been sexually consummated. Indeed many well-intentioned friends and associates offered "cures" for the couple's want of pregnancy. The two politely accepted but privately rejected such advice. The few confidants who knew the truth regarded the modality of such childlessness a praiseworthy and lofty form of asceticism. Such a marriage, they felt, deserved honor. The couple could thus feel free, even supported, in accepting their calls to other avenues. Together they joined the Franciscan order's association for lay persons, the Third Order, thus dedicating themselves to further growth in spirituality and virtue.[20]

Upon receiving his inheritance at the age of twenty-three, Elzéar traveled to Italy without Delphine in order to claim his new lordship there as Count of Ariano. The couple had to live apart for four years but kept in relentless heartfelt communication until she could join him again. At the court of King Robert in Naples, Elzéar was given a charge in the royal army. Though facing some opposition from certain nobles, he won by goodwill the hearts of his Italian subjects, though culturally different from them as a Frenchman. It did not hurt that, promoted to lieutenant, he proved to be an extraordinary, even impassioned, military leader. His army, with the help of another count, expelled from Rome the unpopular Henry VII, who opposed King Robert and was aspiring to become the Holy Roman emperor. Returning to Ariano, Elzéar succeeded in defeating rebellious forces there and restored order.[21] Later in Naples he tutored King Robert's twenty-year-old son, Prince Charles,[22] and was named regent of the territory during the king's absence. Charles was stubborn and difficult to manage. But Elzéar, twelve years older than the prince, was patient and managed by his skillful direction to make a gentleman out of him.[23]

When the king later sent Elzéar as ambassador to Paris in order to arrange for the prince's marriage with a noblewoman, Marie de Valois, Elzéar's affable disposition proved again heartwarming to the local court. But before his departure, he and Delphine tenderly and tearfully hugged,

---

20. Donovan, "Blessed Delphine."
21. Vauchez, *Laity*, 74.
22. Giangrosso, *Saints' Lives*, 14–15.
23. Bernard, *Époux vierges*, 79–80, 83, 87, 111, 116–19, 142–43, 146.

though unknowingly for the last time. They had been together for twenty-four years.[24] While on the mission Elzéar became seriously ill and died.

Delphine deeply mourned the loss of her beloved husband.[25] For several years thereafter she served as a spiritual companion to Queen Sanchia, King Robert's widow. Eventually resettling in France, she became rather reclusive in a large Provençal house there. Although she had servants, she greatly simplified her dress and way of life,[26] determined to eventually embrace a vow of poverty. But her intentions did not precisely take that course.

SAINT FERDINAND III—A ROYAL CHAMPION AND HERO BIGGER THAN LIFE

In 1198, or close to then, León's King Alfonso IX and his wife, Castile's Queen Berenguela, welcomed into their lives the newborn Prince Ferdinand III. Thus two geographical areas of what is now northern Spain became solidified—though not yet politically merged—through the couple's union of hearts. The child's mother, whom he resembled, was the sister of the famed Blanche of Castile. Ferdinand was thus the older cousin of France's King Louis IX, Blanche's son, whose notable life will later be recounted in these pages. But the royal couple of León and Castile subsequently and sadly had to disunite because of a papal mandate declaring the marriage invalid by the eventually discovered fact that the couple was too closely related. The regrettable circumstance however affected legally neither the children's legitimacy nor their rights of royal succession since they were conceived in goodwill.[27] Nonetheless the honorable Queen Berenguela was compelled to return to the castle of her father, King Alfonso VIII of Castile, cousin of her former husband Alfonso IX. Heartbroken, she left behind, in the custody of their father, her four children, among them the young Ferdinand.

But when he was seven his maternal grandfather, the king of Castile, requested that Berenguela's four children be allowed to again live with her. The king of León kindly agreed, to her delight and that of her father. It would now be a medieval case of shared custody. The boy Ferdinand was likewise overjoyed. With no disdain for his father, he simply embraced with enthusiasm the chance for renewed life with his mother. The influence of

---

24. Carr, "St. Elzéar of Sabran."
25. Pettinati, "Beata Delfina di Signe," para. 4.
26. Wikipedia, "Delphine de Sabran," para. 7.
27. Maccono, *Ferdinando III*, 22–23.

Good and Wealthy

Berenguela on the young Ferdinand would be, as we will see in a later chapter, notable and impressive. Wise woman that she was, she also functioned as a confidant and even counselor to her father, the king of Castile.

Ferdinand was a delight to the court, largely at least. He was a handsome young man of admirable character, quite adept at chess, an avid soccer player, and, as time went on, an excellent horseman. Jousts were a frequent entertainment at royal festivals, and he was a champion. By his peers, he was unbeatable and nearly so by the older riders. But the compelling nature of the young prince was apparently a threat to someone. For reasons that are unclear, at the age of seventeen Ferdinand was ordered to return to his father's castle in León, an order that the prince willingly but regrettably heeded.

King Alfonso of León was, on first seeing Ferdinand after years of separation, somewhat disappointed in what to him was the prince's boyish appearance. Others in the court too hesitated to display toward him decorum worthy of the successor to their present king. But King Alfonso readily warmed to his son and told him of the stepsisters who awaited him. Ferdinand welcomed the opportunity with enthusiasm. The two princesses received the handsome blond youth with heartfelt—if not giddy—exuberance. Now it was a medieval version of a blended family. Soon the whole court reveled in his lively spirit and, seeing the sportsman in action, cheered his athleticism. He could wear a full set of amour all day without a sign of fatigue. The young prince's image soon developed literally into one typical of a romanticized hero: the tall, handsome, and strapping ruler/warrior, exemplarily modeling nobility, majesty, elegance, virtue, devotion, judiciousness, and determination. These were features that the Spanish court, citizenry, and chroniclers would admire throughout his royal career.

Rather soon after his sojourn in León, Prince Ferdinand was called back to Castile. His mother's brother, the young King Henry, had died, thus leaving Berenguela as the successor to her father's throne. But it was time for an appreciable change in the Castilian royalty. After initial squabbles over proper lineage, the image of the royal family was enhanced when, in 1217, Ferdinand assumed dominion over Castile in a unique way. It was a grandiose occasion. Having been welcomed with an enthusiastic acclamation, the royal pair—mother and son—entered the church and ascended to the main altar. Bishops presided prominently, and the nave was packed, both with nobles and citizenry from the urban centers. Berenguela proceeded to her throne. After solemn deliberation, and having received the approbation

Notable Living—Remarkable Exemplars of Goodness

of the nobility, she proclaimed before the nobles that she renounced all sovereignty over her domains in favor of Ferdinand. The generous queen, who could have rightfully assumed mandate of the kingdom, had relinquished the royal scepter to her gifted though relatively youthful son. Word of the declaration spread instantaneously. The crowds within and outside the church broke into thunderous applause. Soon afterwards, on a coronation podium erected before the throngs of enthralled and cheerful citizens, Berenguela lifted from her head the royal crown and placed it on the head of the now King Ferdinand III.

Counseled by his sensitive and discerning mother, at the age of twenty he consented to Berenguela's initiative to find him a suitable bride. Whether as son or king, he saw in his mother wisdom and discretion that he greatly respected and admired.[28] Searching for someone both affable and politically appropriate, the queen mother decided upon the wonderfully admirable princess Beatrice, the beautiful daughter of the German King Philip of Swabia. Beatrice was in no way hesitant to accept the proposal. For she had been well informed by reputable personalities about Ferdinand's virtues as both a king and gentleman. With a large entourage of nobles, attendants, and elegant ladies of Beatrice's age, Berenguela welcomed the young princess and quickly won her heart. The queen mother in turn found the princess discreet and sweet. With chivalrous elegance and mature aplomb, Ferdinand happily welcomed his fair and slender future bride, imposing and graceful in her demeanor. As a paragon of virtue, she mirrored her new husband's noble charm; and that hardly went unnoticed by their contemporaries.

Ferdinand adored his young blond wife and queen, treating her with a loving husband's respect and notable affection. The splendid royal couple's nearly sixteen-year happy union flowered with the births of several children, adding a princess and six princes to the royal household.[29] They thoroughly enjoyed these years of youthful contentment. But an illness during a menacing cold November took Beatrice's life; Ferdinand and the children remained lovingly at her side as she slipped away.

Three years later in 1235, counseled by his mother, grieving to see her thirty-nine-year-old son remain a widower, the bereaved king married the likewise admirable Joan de Ponthieu, with whom he had six more children.[30]

---

28. Laurentie, *Saint Ferdinand*, 36, 43.
29. Heckmann, "St. Ferdinand III."
30. Wikipedia, "Joan, Countess of Ponthieu," para. 5; Wikipedia, "Ferdinand III of

Good and Wealthy

The virtuous, intelligent, and beautiful bride had been chosen for him by Berenguela's sister, Blanche of Castile, at Berenguela's request. The wedding was a joyous celebration. Ferdinand grew to love Joan dearly, crowned her as queen, and bade her to accompany him on many of his travels.[31] She was always happy to be close at hand, even when he battled nearby. For the rest of his life, Joan was his constant companion.[32] She therefore would watch more of this alluring king's momentous life unfold.

SAINT MARGARET OF SCOTLAND— A RAVISHING ROYAL BEAUTY

It was a time of terror during the early years of the Danish King Canute's objectionable reign in England. There, a mid-eleventh-century English nobleman came to be known as Edward the Exile because, as a member of a royal household and heir to the British throne, he was banished to northern Europe during Canute's treachery. In later years he found his way to Hungary. There, dear little Princess Margaret was born, about 1045, the daughter of Edward and his wife, Agatha. The couple's close association with the Hungarian King Andrew created for their daughter an environment that was markedly reverential. For the king was a widely respected champion of the royal court's recently adopted Christian faith.

As a young lady, likely around twelve years of age, Margaret and her family returned to a temporarily safe England rightfully ruled by Edward the Confessor, himself later named a saint. Sadly Margaret's father Edward soon died, leaving Margaret and the rest of her family in the care of the Confessor's royal court.[33] But nine years later the family chose to attempt refuge again in continental Europe after the Norman invasion and the establishment of new sovereignty in the island nation. At least one tradition reports that the group was repulsed at sea by a ravaging storm and that the refugee family lost all hope of rescue. Yet the powerful gusts brought the group to Scotland. When folk on the shore reported the incident to Malcolm III, king of the Scots, he became curious about the reported refinement of the stranded group. After learning from his emissaries about

---

Castile," para. 25.

31. Fernández, *King of Castile*, 1–2, 12–17, 26–27, 30, 41–44, 47–51, 63–64, 82–83, 151, 181.

32. Fitzhenry, *Saint Fernando III*, 98–99, 239.

33. McRoberts, *Margaret Queen of Scotland*, sec. 1.

the family's plight, noble King Malcolm, acting like a gentleman, went to meet them and then personally escorted them to his palace. The gesture, generous, though perhaps unanticipated, would be extended—no doubt for reasons that attended and perhaps even heightened gentlemanly generosity.

As warmly welcomed guests of the royal household, Margaret and her family enjoyed the regular company of Malcolm. Familiar to many of later centuries as the character of the same name in Shakespeare's *Macbeth*, the forty-year-old king—likely widowed for the past few years—gazed fondly on the now twenty-four year old Margaret, who was apparently already known to him as a member of an English royal family. Had circumstances permitted, he may have met the pretty, reportedly fair-haired, blue-eyed princess earlier in England and, before his first marriage, considered her as his choice for a wife.[34] Then she was still intent on entering monastic life.[35] Now however the time for lovingly pursuing her was more propitious, and the beautiful Margaret captured his heart for good. She reciprocated sincerely, acceding to love as virtuous though far less cloistered than that of her youth. The wedding, with a bishop presiding,[36] was a magnificent celebration, full of splendor and color beyond Scottish precedent.[37] The Scots of the time were not as lavish in their festivities as the English. The impact of the nuptials was dramatic. The couple's vows initiated a discernible and gratifying evolution in Scottish culture.

The couple's marriage was strong and marked by notable affection.[38] They loved each other passionately. One of the ways by which the king displayed his esteem for Margaret was to consent to their naming the children after members of her family rather than his.[39] With Malcolm she had two daughters and six sons, three of whom eventually became kings of Scotland, as, because of deaths, the succession passed from one brother to another.[40] Besides honoring Margaret's designs for her children, the king further displayed his love with gifts and fond embraces. He was not a perfect husband however. He could at times be unruly, even unkind. But Queen Margaret stood by him with a tenderness and patience that soothed his soul. And

---

34. Huddleston, "St. Margaret of Scotland"; Keene, *St. Margaret*, 42–43.
35. Wilson, *St. Margaret*, 60, 64, 73.
36. Menzies, *St. Margaret*, 19, 41.
37. Marshall, "Malcolm Canmore," para. 11.
38. Keene, *Saint Margaret*, 30, 50.
39. Dunlop, *Queen Margaret of Scotland*, 37, 46, 50.
40. Wikipedia, "Saint Margaret of Scotland," para. 9.

over the years of royal life, her warm dedication would overflow to many others besides her husband.

SAINT LOUIS IX—AN ACCOMPLISHED RULER WITH AN ASSERTIVE MOTHER

Born in 1214, he was only twelve years old when his father, King Louis VIII of France, died. As an infant member of the noble household, the prince had been baptized in a castle at Poissy just west of Paris. Now the royal tween would be crowned King Louis IX in the great cathedral of Rheims, which hovered in the country's northeast. Since he was not yet old enough to rule effectively, his mother, Blanche of Castile, functioned as his regent. As we have already noted, she was the sister of the Castilian Queen Berenguela. Though not a native of France, Blanche wielded her queenly authority effectively, with force and precision both domestically and internationally, adding significantly to the stature of the kingdom. She was a woman with well-earned stature.

Her attention to detail marked her influence on the young king's education, one indeed befitting royalty. She engaged for him tutors in the Latin language, oratory, literary composition, military tactics, and governance. When he was nineteen, Blanche determined that he would marry Marguerite of Provence. She was only thirteen then, but the arrangement accorded with the social usage and political expediency of the times.

Since in those days romantic love was practically unknown by couples in arranged marriages, it might well have been that the king's initial sentiments toward his nubile wife were rather reserved. More than aloof at times, he could be moody and even argumentative, like a lanky youngster still unsure of himself. Maturity however suffered no long delay. His later caring attention to Marguerite showed without question how he grew to love dearly the girl he had originally not sought, the bride chosen for him.

Her father had provided a generous dowry, and the wedding took place southeast of Paris in the majestic Sens Cathedral. Nobility flavored the whole celebration; ladies, gentlemen, and clergy—from near and afar—abounded. Before an admiring throng outside the cathedral, and in the presence of the archbishop, the marriage was sealed by the couple's joining of hands and the king's solemnly placing the ring on Marguerite's finger. Then, inside the crowded cathedral, their marriage was solemnized with a splendorous Mass.

There followed the next day a lavish coronation of the new queen. They were a poster couple. As during their courtship, throughout their thirty-six years of marriage they were able to display warm regard for one another, a steadiness that ran deep. She esteemed his kingliness, and he admired his wife as the nation's fitting queen. Indeed only established habits occasionally caused annoyance. The king, for example, could be volatile or harsh.[41] Sanctity does not preclude fault but does include repentance. The saintly king had his limits, as he himself well knew and confessed.

Louis and Marguerite had much in common. She was decidedly religious, a feature quite dear to him; and together they enjoyed riding, literature, and music. They were thus undaunted by the regularly intentional interference of the king's mother, who, despite her many virtues, did not hide a kind of antagonism for Marguerite; perhaps it was jealousy of the beautiful queen, or mistrust of Marguerite's political loyalties. Blanche had yielded to Louis's leadership of the kingdom when he married, but she remained a force behind the scenes all her years. The young queen Marguerite did not take her mother-in-law's aversion personally. When Blanche died in 1252, Marguerite was sincerely mournful, deeply sympathetic of the king's sorrow.

With Marguerite, Louis enjoyed the births of eleven children, though two of them died in childhood, and another as a teen. Louis engaged tutors for his children's education but also taught them himself, employing both historical and moral lessons. He fervently desired that his children enter various religious orders but was respectful of their own designs. All of them remained in the lay state and married.[42]

The nearly four decades of the king's reign, as we will see, were marked by monumental social, political, military, and religious activity. Louis was a man of unfailing energy, common sense, humor, and humility. Such vibrancy and productivity will become increasingly evident.

VENERABLE PIERRE TOUSSAINT—FREELY A SLAVE

His title, "venerable," specifies someone credibly designated and formally declared a person with saint-like qualities. It thus proclaims a well-founded hope that such a renowned and revered individual will in due time be officially declared a saint. This is the story of such a man.

---

41. Le Goff, *Saint Louis*, 87–89, 596–97.
42. Richard, *St. Louis*, 1–8, 251.

Good and Wealthy

Ten years before the colonists issued their Declaration of Independence from England but far from Philadelphia, where the document's infamous signatures launched a new American era, a little black baby came unobtrusively into another part of the world. In 1766 his cries sweetly pierced the air on an impressive sector of St. Domingue, the Caribbean island now called Haiti. Its plantations yielded profusely the bulk of wares that France, the island's colonial lord, traded internationally. The newborn was distinct however. Though legally a slave, he was the grandson of his master's deeply respected freed slave woman. Since she remained in the household as an appointed servant, baby Pierre belonged to a family of highly regarded domestic servants, though kin to seven hundred thousand of African origin who, with their toil and pain, stoked the economy of their oppressors' homeland across the Atlantic.

Such laborers were underlings tragically answerable to a handful of French masters who drove them mercilessly. Whipping and sundry other unspeakable forms of torture typically kept such anguished workers submissive and productive. Their joints ached and their blood flowed in service of their masters' profit.

The baby however was one of the fortunate few whose masters disdained slavery's abominations. Abhorred and ridiculed by most of his peers, this particular proprietor of a large northern plantation wielded authority with respect for those who attended to the chores, including Pierre's father, who was a field slave. The master welcomed the ability of Pierre's grandmother to read and write, having apparently taught her himself. His daughter served as the baby's godmother. And since she was only five (a common age for plantation godparents), she would soon become one of his several playmates. As the slave baby Pierre Toussaint grew, he learned from his grandmother how to read and write and was even permitted to enter the library of the lordly mansion to enrich his mind and imagination. And the boy was eager to learn. He was possibly being groomed to be a valet and butler and to one day be a fair-minded manager on the plantation. Young Pierre blossomed in the light of his knowledge and in the faith he acquired and developed in the household. He was a gentle, playful, and heartwarming child, and a fine actor, often delighting everyone on the plantation with his impersonations.

Meantime, in nightly bands, multitudes of his less fortunate peers shattered the nocturnal gloom with their painful longing for freedom. Stoked by ritual and prayer of their native land, the fire of liberty burning inside them would lead to violent revolution. Within a decade nearly two million blacks and almost a quarter million whites would succumb to brutal mutual slaughter. Abhorrence at these atrocities likely influenced Pierre's later admonition that bloodshed not stain the abolitionist movement in America.

Hoping to find refuge from St. Domingue's swelling storm, the son of Pierre's original master—and now the inheritor and new master of the estate—moved his household, including Pierre and his sister, to New York City. The move was designed to last only until the turmoil in the homeland abated. So the rest of Pierre's family, including his father, stayed behind on the island, presumably to fare well in light of the rebels' goodwill toward them.

The newly arriving family was among many French-speaking settlers whom New Yorkers welcomed into their prominent social and political circles where the prevailing languages were both English and French. These former colonists, including famed military heroes who by their revolution were now inhabitants of their own land, felt kinship with the French, whose armies had aided them in their war for freedom. In two more years this city would become the first capital of the new union of states where plurality marked unity. When that era came, it is said, probably apocryphally, Pierre was busy at his work but could hear the roars of the crowd at George Washington's inauguration, and he could later see the new leader outside the presidential home. At Alexander Hamilton's funeral procession, Pierre would be among the spectators. He would also observe Thomas Jefferson dutifully attending a church wedding.[43]

Pierre would become neither an ordinary citizen nor an outsider. Because of his color, he belonged to a minority among whites; because he was Catholic, he belonged as well to a minority among Protestants. But disparagement for such distinctions would rapidly diminish, even considerably. Pierre's young master, the original master's son, was now treating him in New York more like a brother than a slave. He arranged for Pierre to become an apprentice to one of New York's highly regarded hairdressers. At the time, stylizing intricate and grandiose coiffures required highly refined skills and was one of the few professions accessible to blacks. The twenty-something Pierre soon became a master himself, a skilled artisan, unrivaled in his trade, who earned impressive payments from the city's fashion-minded, including Alexander Hamilton's wife and their granddaughter. He

---

43. Tarry, *Pierre Toussaint*, 112, 168.

was advancing admirably in his use of English, which his master had already begun to teach him in St. Domingue. By his financial status he would become well qualified to vote.[44] But he permanently remained a French citizen, though legally a resident of the United States.[45]

Within a short time his master, hoping to retrieve the threatened plantation, hurriedly returned to St. Domingue only to die there, as his lavish property, like that of all the other colonial occupants, succumbed to the widespread, successful and gruesomely blood-stained revolution on the island. As it became clear that there would be no returning to the island and no inheritance for the master's widow, Pierre, now with substantial income from some of the most notable families in the city, assumed financial responsibility for her. At the same time he generously and openly served as her slave so that she could maintain her dignity in social circles. His enslavement now was a freely chosen servitude, though not the indentured sort since he bore no financial burden to his apparent owner. In fact, scarcely few knew—or discreetly pretended not to know—that he was essentially his household's provider. He saw his legally designated "owner" through a series of misfortunes. And close to death she formally granted him his freedom.[46]

Though an advocate of causes on behalf of blacks, his participation in the raging debate over slavery was quite reserved. He valued the freedom he had obtained, and he bought the freedom of both his eventual wife Juliette and his enslaved aunt. He did not however overtly link arms with New York's abolitionists. By his reasoning it was far better for him to do what he could to improve the lives of others than to be confrontational. When a law was passed emancipating the children of slaves, he declined to parade any jubilation, lamenting that he simply could not rejoice as long as so many of those still enslaved elsewhere were dying for their freedom. He did suggest however that the use of violence to achieve abolition should be avoided at all costs. When the plight of fugitive southern slaves came to his attention, he provided help. As to one group's goodwill objective of sending those of African heritage back to their ancestral homeland, he was politely dismissive.

Once emancipated, he rejoiced in marrying his dear Juliette. Though she was several years younger, her lively spirit matched his own, and he

---

44. African American Registry, "Pierre Toussaint," para. 7.
45. Jones, *Pierre Toussaint*, 6–7, 29, 54, 82–83, 157, 163, 215, 323.
46. Sheehan and Odell, *Pierre Toussaint*, 8, 12, 44, 62, 83.

relished in the beauty of his multiracial St. Domingan love. The couple established a third-floor New York apartment as their new home. Juliette was happy and unstinting as Pierre's partner in managing the household.[47] Below them lived his onetime owner's cook, nurse, and second husband. Their household was still dependent on Pierre and his young wife for financial support.[48] But the newlyweds' kindness to others would not stop here. Their ensuing years together would be dramatically marked by uncommon generosity.

BLESSED FRÉDÉRIC OZANAM—A RENOWNED SCHOLAR WITH A TENDER HEART

To his contemporaries he was a man of piety and outstanding dedication. He is not yet officially a saint but is on track to becoming one, and deservedly so. Evidence of his holiness, and of widespread devotion to him, has thus far brought him the title "blessed," an official designation which immediately precedes that of "saint." The latter title would bring greater renown to the extraordinary qualities of his life and achievements.

In 1813, when the French occupied the Italian city of Milan, Jean-Antoine Ozanam served as a captain in the Napoleonic army but soon retired to become a medical doctor. In that same year he and his wife Marie became the parents of Frédéric, the second youngest of four children who would survive beyond infancy. After Napoleon's defeat in 1815 the couple returned to Lyon, France, where Antoine practiced in a local hospital. Frédéric greatly admired his father, considering him an inspiring model of perseverance, faith, and charity. Antoine regularly tended to the poor of the local slums, typically providing medical services without charge. Such generosity would characterize his whole lifetime, and that of his wife.

Marie was a good mother and also gave generous attention to the poor. Young Frédéric, meek and adorable, received a good deal of maternal attention from her as well as his older sister. But with the latter's untimely death at nineteen, seven-year-old Frédéric became what he later regarded as strong-willed and rebellious, likely exhibiting temporary signs of grief. A hoped-for antidote to his turmoil was enrollment in a local school where his mind could flourish and his heart heal. Though by his own admission lazy at times, as someone who learned quickly, he proved the experiment

47. Lee, *Memoir of Pierre Toussaint*, 3–4, 80.
48. Hanley, "Pierre Toussaint," para. 62.

successful by brilliantly excelling in his classes, especially those in languages and literature.

Relying on his academic learning and heightened interest in his faith, he turned to writing and soon succeeded in publishing articles that became widely recognized as substantive reflections on his religion. This was the beginning of a lifelong pursuit of truth and justice. His unwavering intent was to correct false representations of Christianity, not to defend the several dishonorable authorities who had marked it historically. Moving on to studies as a university student of law in Paris, he received from a prominent scholar support for his views. Thus emboldened he formed a discussion group of fellow Christians to consider ways to counter widespread anti-religious sentiment, especially as it was voiced, frequently and vigorously, by his professors. The group confronted their teachers with rational argumentation, and even in one case persuaded a professor to refrain from cants against faith or religion. Somewhat later Frédéric helped to form a larger group with similar views. Participants of various persuasions, including nonbelievers, became engaged. Soon various Christian members of the group added social action to their engagement by aiding the poor of the area. Frédéric continued his studies until eventually earning the degree of doctor of laws.

Desiring to assist his parents in their old age, he returned to Lyon and began to practice law. When his father died from a tragic fall, Frédéric assumed the financial responsibility for his mother and much younger brother. He accomplished this at first by tutoring in law, then by classroom teaching. He emphasized social concerns and current problems related to law. Meantime his love of literary works and history prompted him to attain a second doctoral degree in literature at Paris' prestigious Sorbonne. Now his lectures in law were peppered with historical, philosophical, and literary references. Audiences overflowed the auditoriums and relished in his acumen, flourish, and wit.

With a soaring professional life in Lyon, and competency in three classical languages and four modern ones, Frédéric returned to the Sorbonne and assumed a prominent professorate in foreign literature. He was now twenty-seven-years old. Though a successful professor, the call he felt to charitable work remained strong, to such a degree that he considered becoming a priest. He clearly had a high regard for marriage, both psychologically and spiritually. But, he wondered, could married life accord with heartfelt service to the poor? A former teacher and counselor, himself a

Notable Living—Remarkable Exemplars of Goodness

priest, convinced Frédéric that it could. The clergyman even subtly through a "chance" meeting introduced him to a lovely young lady. She found his ardent religiousness and warm generosity eminently attractive. Smitten by her tenderness and charm, he called her smile a "ray of happiness."[49] The following year Frédéric, at twenty-eight, married twenty-one year-old Amélie Soulacroix in a joy-filled church. He was brought to tears by the ceremony, which appeared to him as the touch of heaven.[50] It was not long before he became persuaded that the rewards of marriage in fact energized his scholarly and charitable competencies. He eventually became convinced that, generally speaking, marriage and the family, more than individualism, were of fundamental importance for a healthy society.

The couple was extremely happy. Frédéric celebrated their union by sending Amélie flowers on every anniversary of their marriage and by dedicating to her a number of affectionate poems. He called her lovingly his dove, flower, or pearl. He seems to have had some reservations about his readiness for dancing but assured her of his willingness to learn in order to increase her happiness.[51] After the pair moved to Paris, Amélie endured a number of miscarriages. But in 1841 their daughter Marie was born. Frédéric was a proud and dedicated father.[52] Marie brought warmth and light to the couple's apartment near Paris' famous Luxembourg Gardens. From his youth Frédéric had been a lover of nature. So the proximity of gardens with their meticulously crafted lanes and delightfully displayed plants afforded numerous enjoyable family walks. Alternate alluring routes included the Tuileries Garden and the Champs Élysées.[53]

But over the years his laborious preparation of lectures, his meticulous research, abundant writing, and continued charitable activity took their toll. Amélie provided him with unflagging support.[54] And he cherished her for guiding and sustaining him in all that he accomplished.[55] Reduced to near inactivity at the age of thirty-four, he was forced into an extended rest through a sojourn in Italy. Even away from his routine however, he was

---

49. Baunard, *His Correspondence*, 185.
50. Ozanam, *Letters*, 269.
51. Harrison, *Romantic Catholics*, 206, 211–12, 216–17, 221.
52. Rybolt, "Virtuous Personality," 36, 40–42.
53. Cholvy, *Christianisme a besoin*, 207, 210, 223.
54. Scott, "Frédéric Ozanam," 33–34, 37, 42, 44.
55. Sickinger, *Antoine Frédéric Ozanam*, 85, 88, 90, 140–41, 196–97.

tantalized by documents that he discovered there. These led him to new insights and to a new book on poetry of the Middle Ages.

Rather revived, he returned with his family to Paris in 1847 only to find a new and demanding challenge. With the recent establishment of France's Second Republic, friends persuaded him to run for public office. His campaign was based on innovative ideas that would later become standard fare of varying political ideologies. But the voters rejected his proposals as too progressive, and he thenceforth never returned directly into politics. But during the next few years the stress of rejection continued as the Catholic Party, members of his own church, scorned his ideas. His burden was multiplied by an ever-increasing workload of teaching and research at the university, by the exhaustion of continued publications, and by ongoing work with the Society of St. Vincent de Paul, established with his efforts during his student days.

While attempting to profit from a much needed period of respite on the French coast in 1851, he visited the Great Exhibition, the historic industrial fair in London. But Frédéric was more moved with compassion for the plight of Irish refugees there than by excitement over the unprecedented marvels filling the exhibition's venue, the Crystal Palace. Soon he was able to return to lecturing—and most powerfully—at the Sorbonne. But only a few months later he was struck with a devastating fever and pleurisy. Nonetheless he was able to heed the request of a friend, France's Education Minister, to do some research in Italy. The official undoubtedly hoped that it would lift Frédéric's spirits and perhaps energize him physically. In Pisa he was in fact able to do some profitable research and provide helpful guidance to the Society of St. Vincent de Paul there. Despite his continued discomfort, the sojourn was typical of his lifelong faith and dedication.[56] The scholar with the tender heart would leave his mark on history, and quite a mark it would be.

BLESSED VICTOIRE RASOAMANARIVO—A ROYAL CHAMPION OF THE OPPRESSED

In the Indian Ocean and just to the east of southern Africa lies the vast island of Madagascar with its majestic mountains and richly diverse forestry. The nineteenth century saw the area's fifteen black African tribes unite under monarchial rule and designate the newly named Antananarivo as its

---

56. Slattery, *Blessed Frederic Ozanan*, 3–13.

capital. There, in 1848, the baby girl, then named Rasoamanarivo, was born into one of the wealthiest families on the island. Her grandfather had been the queen's prince consort and commander of the royal army. As a child Rasoamanarivo was easygoing and mild mannered. Having entered a religious school and converted in early adolescence from her ancestral religion to Catholicism, she proudly added Victoire to her name. Soon she entered an arranged marriage with a cousin. Blood relationship with a spouse was common for someone of her social status, but the marriage nonetheless required an ecclesiastical dispensation, which was granted.[57] Thus she took her place among the courtiers and their royal environment.

During the early months of the marriage she preferred to spend more time continuing her education than participating in the leisure and fashion of the court. A more refined courtly manner would come in time, exhibiting more her diplomacy than pleasure. Though she had earlier been attracted to vowed religious life, she eventually saw the wisdom of her marriage, considering what influence it allowed her to have on developments in Madagascar's Christian population. Sadly her husband notoriously drank far beyond measure and burdened their relationship by his abusive behavior. He frequently failed to appear for dinner—sometime for days or weeks—and needed fellow revelers to help his inebriated strides find their crooked way home. Nonetheless she remained loyal to him during their twenty-four years together, prayed for his reform, sought prayers for him, and invited him to activities where he could experience others' joy in being Christian.

He could not help, at times and begrudgingly, being moved by what appeared to him as tender traps, to such an extent that he would then let himself be subjected to kneeling with her as she prayed, or to contributing to one of her charities, or to helping her deliver goods to the needy. At the same time she unflinchingly and dutifully fulfilled her social and sometimes obsequious obligations as a member of the court. There her religiosity, though at first provoking surprise and even mockery in the essentially Protestant milieu, eventually earned her respect and admiration. Gradually her stalwart spirituality would transfigure into engagement on behalf of her church and nation, and thus become widely inspirational beyond the royal palace. She became a champion of the poor and financially supported the building of churches. When the local government began to place restraints on activities of the French present throughout the island, all French

---

57. Unienville, *Victoire Rasoamanarivo*, paras. 9, 16, 25.

missionaries were recalled to their homeland. At the same time the eighty thousand Catholics now bereft of priests and nuns maintained a sense of kinship with the remaining French and were regarded as traitors. Before his departure, one of the missionaries had entrusted the faithful to the care of a lay organization which he enjoined Victoire to guide. She humbly accepted her new mission, thus eminently enhancing her status as a Christian leader.

One of her first achievements was to secure the reopening of the churches, which had been officially barred and guarded. Impressed by her fortitude and spiritual example, members of the congregation pleaded with her to sit in their midst, in the center of the church and in a specially decorated pew, rather than inconspicuously on the side. Not that official Catholic worship was occurring anywhere on the island. But some devotions could be offered without clergy. The lay leadership organized Sunday gatherings and religious education. The churches abounded with prayers, hymns, and preaching,[58] all effected with great dignity and devotion by laypersons appropriately prepared. Though Catholicism had not been officially banned, persecution in fact prevailed as many teachers incurred imprisonment. One of Victoire's uncles was among the governmental antagonists.

Yet she offered to all those oppressed her heartfelt support and encouragement. Arguing forcefully that religious devotion and loyal citizenship are compatible, she asserted that for her and her fellow believers, it was not merely a matter of compatibility but of firm enduring commitment in both areas. Madagascar was their country, the one they wholeheartedly embraced and loved. By her intervention many were spared prosecution.

When, after three years the missionaries were free to return to the island, Victoire could give more attention to the queen, but only with some reservation; her interests were more spiritual.[59] In the midst of her continued charitable activities, her husband incurred a fatal injury. He had fallen drunkenly from a gallery to a floor below. Feeling his life quickly draining, he listened to Victoire's tender invitation to repent and believe. With a fervent murmur he turned to God and confessed his Christian faith, the faith that his wife of twenty-five years had so beautifully modeled for him.[60] With a newfound spirit he lived for five days before his end was evident.[61] Victoire called for a priest. But with none available, Victoire, by

---

58. Razafy-Andriamihaingo, "Victoire Rasoamanarivo," paras. 4–18.

59. Ramahery, *Ange Visible*, 88.

60. Fourcadier, *Vie Héroïque*, 23, 55–58, 68, 72, 83–84, 99.

61. Simon-Perret, *Victoire Rasoamanarivo*, 39, 56, 58–60, 62, 136–37.

acceptable church practice, baptized her dying spouse herself just before he died. Retreating into long-term mourning, she was seen less and less in the royal court. In exchange for her palatial wardrobe, she donned the simple appearance of a widow as expected in the island's culture, braided hair and a dress of modest colors.[62] For six more years, in ever-deteriorating health she nonetheless continued her spiritual and charitable practices. Her final moments found her terribly weakened but rapt in prayer.[63] Her legacy, of which much more will be told, would be unforgettable.

SAINTS LOUIS AND MARIE-AZÉLIE MARTIN— AN INDUSTRIOUS AND DEDICATED COUPLE

Louis, born in 1823 and named in honor of France's great saintly king, was one of five children but the only one to survive into adulthood. As a typical child of a military family, he grew up in various locations and attended many different schools, all however in his native France. His parents, warmly devoted in the practice of their faith, raised him and his siblings accordingly. Though initially attracted to monastic life, he eventually left his Burgundian town and in Alençon took up clock making, watchmaking and jewelry sales, a career nurtured by his penchant for artistry. The quaint town, with its medieval architecture and the Gothic splendor of its Notre-Dame Church, had been his father's choice for retirement when Louis was still a boy. For the older Louis it became again a welcoming home. In his attractive shop he enjoyed a profitable trade. For leisure he relished his favorite sport of fishing. Eventually he was able to purchase a somewhat small but charming house with a garden that, owing to his love of nature, he manicured meticulously.

His eventual wife was the pretty and energetic Marie-Azélie Guérin (Zélie). Born in 1831 as one of three children, she, like Louis, had grown up in a military family firm in the practice of its faith and whose father had brought the family to Alençon for his retirement. There she received an excellent education, particularly in literature, which helps account for the fine style and charm of the many letters she wrote to Louis and other members of her family. She felt in her younger years that she wanted to become a nun but later decided to learn the fine artistry of lacemaking

---

62. Unienville, *Victoire Rasoamanarivo*, paras. 18–20; Simon-Perret, *Victoire Rasoamanarivo*, 139.

63. Marie, "August 6, 2014."

in order to supplement the family's rather modest retirement income and to prepare for whatever marriage would be in store for her. One day her industrious life was enriched by what was practically love at first sight. She had been strolling across a bridge in Alençon when an attractive and elegant man caught her eye. He seemed to be approaching her quizzically. A voice inside her gave assurance that this was one to marry. And indeed he was. Their extraordinary attraction to one another was immediate, and it showed. After a brief courtship they exchanged their marital vows amid the ancient arches of Alençon's Notre Dame church. It was 1858; she was twenty-six and he thirty-five.

Initially they were abstinent sexually because of their religiously tempered appreciation of perpetual virginity. Espousing a long-established marital custom still common at the time, they felt that they could enjoy their deep love for one another while fervently satisfying their spiritual desires. Their forebears, Elzéar and Delphine, had proved this—as we have seen—centuries ago. Thus the first addition to the Martin couple's home was a foster child, a little boy whose widowered father could not properly care for him. The child was with them for ten months,[64] much to their pleasure. With that experience they soon decided that it would be an additional blessing to have their own children by birth.[65] It was hardly a decision without commitment. Of their subsequent nine children only five—all daughters—would live beyond infancy or early childhood. At the age of forty-one Zélie would bear the last child, Therese, who would later become revered as a saint. Giving young ones life and support brought the couple immense happiness, drawing them even closer to each other.[66] Not that their devotion to family was without trials. Because she had difficulty breast feeding, Zélie's already active life was stressed by frequent, rather lengthy trips to visit one of her young ones left temporarily with a wet nurse. And the couple endured particular hardship when an employee verbally abused one of their little girls.[67]

Zélie had opened her own business, which became so successful that Louis eventually found it more profitable to give up his craft and to sell his profitable concern in favor of becoming her partner in lacemaking. But the life of the otherwise happy family would be sorrowfully reconfigured with

---

64. Cadéot, *Zélie Martin*, 23, 39.
65. Office of the Postulator General of the Discalced Carmelites, "Profile."
66. Louis Wust and Marjorie Wust, *Louis Martin*, 43–44, 67.
67. Ziegler, "History Awaits," paras. 18–19.

Zélie's death in 1877. Having lost his partner in trade, Louis was able to profitably sell their successful business and pleasant home in order to move to Lisieux with his five daughters, including the four-year-old Therese. It was hard for him to leave his longtime home and friends in Alençon.[68] But with the counsel of his girls he agreed that it would be better to be closer to relatives. The Martin family was thus welcomed by Louis's brother-in-law, Isidore Guérin, who ran a pharmacy there.[69] Isidore's business was prospering, his wife was generously disposed to provide maternal care for the Martin girls, and he was able to accommodate the family in a comfortable residence adjoining his own. Eventually the Martins found a pleasant permanent house nearby. This would be the family home for the next twelve years.[70] Here Louis created a nest where he could continue to rear and nurture his five daughters with the love, as one of them put it, of both a mother and a father.[71] As a single parent he excelled. The Martin family, as will be further clarified, had always lived exemplarily, dutifully remaining steadfast in face of trials. And this latest challenge was not the last for Louis.

SAINT GIANNA BERETTA MOLLA—GENEROSITY BEYOND MEASURE

In 1922 the Italian town of Magenta, a suburb of Milan, saw the birth of a baby girl destined for an edifying life. One of eight children who survived beyond infancy, little Gianna brought warmth and joy to the simple home of Maria and Alberto Beretta. Gianna's family moved about thirty miles northeast to Bergamo when she was three and then to Genoa when she was fifteen, only to return to Bergamo when she was nineteen. She struggled with her studies during her earliest years in school but eventually earned grades fine enough to earn her an exemplary graduation.[72] Her younger days were also marked by the joys of hiking, a love of painting, and deftness at the piano. By commitments to various service movements she demonstrated refined leadership capacities. Her intelligence became evident

---

68. Di Nicola and Danese, *Amore scritto in cielo*, 39–40, 46, 49, 62–63, 152.

69. Wikipedia, "Louis Martin and Marie-Azélie Guérin," para. 8.

70. Piat, *Story of a Family*, 3–46, 262–64; Louis Wust and Marjorie Wust, *Louis Martin*, 150, 154.

71. Cadéot, *Louis Martin*, 41, 69–70.

72. Guerriero, introduction to *Journey of Our Love*, 6–7.

through her later success in medical school, though earlier her studies had been interrupted for a year because of illness.[73]

Having received her medical degree, she opened an office in Mesero, just west of Milan. As a physician and surgeon she attended to her patients with devotion. Her humanitarian instincts were especially evident when she offered treatment without compensation. Her office, and thus her daily routines, were within the view of one Pietro Molla, a successful engineer and officer in a nearby firm that was a prominent stimulus to the local economy.

It was not exactly love at first sight when she first encountered him. They had met quite casually in social and business settings where he, unknown to her, was quite attracted by her charm and professionalism. His infatuation would become love beyond measure, and soon he won her heart. He was ten years older than her and likewise dedicated to humanitarian service. Their sense of kinship amplified by profound love was mutual. Each wanted more than anything else to make the other happy. That they were meant for each other was eminently evident. On their marriage day in 1955, when Gianna entered the church on the arm of her brother, the congregation burst into relentless confirmatory applause during her entire walk down the aisle.[74] Meantime the tower's bells acclaimed soaring accolades of their own.[75]

The couple's expectations for marriage were fulfilled with happiness and offspring. Within the next two years they joyfully welcomed into their home a baby boy and then a baby girl. Both children had health issues, which the dedicated parents attended to with loving devotion.[76] Another little girl came two years later. Gianna endured two miscarriages before conceiving again in 1961. This stabler pregnancy was however complicated by the presence of a dangerous tumor in Gianna's uterus.[77] Such a shadow over the happy family would have tragic consequences. Her story and that of her family would be sad but edifying.

---

73. Wikipedia, "Gianna Beretta Molla," para. 5.
74. Brown, *No Greater Love*, 20.
75. Pelucchi, *Saint Gianna*, 63–64, 74.
76. Burke, "Saint Gianna Beretta Molla," paras. 14–17.
77. Pastoral Centre, "Life of St. Gianna Beretta Molla," paras. 33–37.

BLESSEDS LUIGI AND MARIA BELTRAME QUATTROCCHI—AN EXTRAORDINARY COUPLE EXTRAORDINARILY IN LOVE

It was 1880. In the shadow of majestic Mt. Etna, newborn Luigi Beltrame breathed the air of eastern Sicily. At a young age he was adopted by his maternal aunt and uncle, who were childless. Though in regular contact with his birth family, his fondness for his adopted parents inclined him to add their surname, Quattrocchi, to his before they moved with him to Rome. Somewhat to the north in Italy's Florence, the boisterous and temperamental Corsini couple had welcomed their little Maria into the world. The year was 1884. Her childhood years, spent in her hometown and later in Rome, were marked by her regular diplomatic efforts to calm her parents' argumentative dispositions. Such concern abetted her maturation and augmented her strength of character.

Though from rather different backgrounds, Maria and Luigi found their ways to one another through common interests. Luigi studied law, earning a university degree and acquiring a faculty position at his alma mater. Besides teaching, he would pursue an impressive professional career, providing legal counsel for important private and governmental agencies, serving on several bank boards, and eventually acquiring prominent and respected Italian civil service positions. He refused however to become a member of Mussolini's National Fascist Party.

As a prolific author Maria would become a widely esteemed educator, particularly of youth.[78] Her star would align with Luigi's in Rôme after their student years when their families became acquainted. She was seventeen; he was twenty-one. It was friendship at first sight and soon romance beyond words.[79] The youthful, vibrant Maria and the easygoing Luigi were one another's first and only loves, so treasuring their initial confessions of undying affection that they would celebrate the occasion every year thereafter. Throughout their lives their many letters to one another would abound in profound sentiment and charming literary flair. The young starry-eyed couple dated for some three years,[80] then love's might inevitably led them to marriage early in their twenties.

---

78. O'Neel, *Thirty-Nine New Saints*, 131.
79. Catapano and Angrisani, *Mistica coniugale*, 17, 20–21.
80. Vatican News, "Luigi e Maria," para. 16.

Theirs was a tender, passionate love disposed for—but not yet showing signs of—sanctity. They honeymooned in southern Italy and Sicily. The fledgling couple lived for a time in the same house as Maria's family. Proximity to her parents and grandparents fared well. Maria was an engaging conversationalist. All in the household enjoyed their companionship even as the newlyweds relished in their own common interests, burdened only by Luigi's regular travel, for which they compensated through their warm correspondence.

Within a year they rejoiced in the birth of their first son. New home life and parental generosity brought the pair's relinquishment of accustomed familiarity with the latest in culture and the arts. Feeling rather exhausted and sometimes lonely whenever Luigi was away, Maria wondered if she could suitably endure when she learned she was pregnant again. She was plagued too, like many a new mother, by doubts about meeting the little ones' many needs. But an air of contentment ensued with the arrival of an infant girl. Maria gained heartening confidence, and Luigi provided exceptional support. Fewer than two years later, and after a problematic delivery, the couple delighted in the birth of their third child and second son.

Four years after that Maria was pregnant again. This time serious and daunting circumstances bode Maria's certain death in carrying the child to term. When their gynecologist, a prominent and respected one, vehemently suggested that her life could be spared only by terminating the pregnancy, the couple unhesitatingly refused. By Catholic Church teachings the procedure was allowable since the loss of the fetus would be an indirect and undesired consequence of the suggested medical procedure. But from the couple's perspective, even such an approach amounted to an unacceptable killing of a child in the womb. After four months of Maria's bed rest and the family's unremitting anguish, Maria became disturbingly weak. At that, a month before term, the doctor induced labor and birth. Into the family came another little girl, who, with her mother, survived despite the odds, though Maria also had to overcome anemia and a long postpartum infection.[81]

As the years passed, Maria used her intellectual gifts to write books and articles on matters pertaining to motherhood and family life. At times Luigi lent an editorial hand in her literary productivity. She also participated in charitable activities and traveled with Luigi as they attended to the

---

81. Beltrame Quattrocchi, *Lui, Lei, Noi, Loro*, 23, 27, 69, 73, 76–77, 80–81, 83–84, 89.

sick who sought comfort and healing through devotions at shrines such as that at Lourdes in France.

Having won first place in an Italian law competition, Luigi, with proven administrative skills, served in several highly responsible governmental positions, including Italy's counsel general.[82] With Maria he would be at the service of his family, church, and country in countless ways. The couple would live through historic times, seeing the occupation of Italy during World Wars I and II, and participating thereafter in their nation's reconstruction.[83] Their lives were marked by countless personal and public achievements, of which much more will be said.

---

82. Marie, "April 8, 2008," para. 2.
83. Savior.org, "Blessed Luigi Beltrame Quattrocchi," para. 12.

CHAPTER 2

Contours of Possession— Pleasures of Wealth

The personalities who in these pages are presented as good and wealthy enjoyed prominent or longtime prosperity. Most even lived lavishly. This chapter recounts the extent and nature of their riches, goods, and property that could have captured their undivided attention and lured them away from their spiritual quests, from indeed their attainment of astounding virtue. What they owned however, and what they enjoyed, was hardly enough to disrupt their inspiring journeys. In the midst of treasure, their hearts were also elsewhere. And in every case, a conspicuous amount of treasure there was.

SAINT GUNTRAM—BATHED IN OPULENCE

This scandalous young noble, prone to maliciousness and philandering, eventually did his sixth-century Burgundian kingdom proud. King Guntram was raised in the plush surroundings of early French, or Frankish, royalty. The family estate was luxurious and huge, hugged by sumptuous forests that seemed to breed opulence. The royal palace, resembling little a military fortress or castle, reflected more the architectural artistry of bold columns and arches radiating the strength of stone and the warmth of carved wood. From this central and sprawling residence, the king could gaze out unto the finely crafted surrounding quarters of his officials; among these structures as well were the sturdy lodges of vassals and others with fealty to the king. Somewhat contrasting were the less imposing structures of the many servants and artisans who contributed to the palace's elegance:

Contours of Possession—Pleasures of Wealth

blacksmiths, goldsmiths, cloth makers, and the like. Further out were the homes of herders and farm hands who provided for the royal table. Thus from a young age Guntram knew and fully enjoyed fine food and palatial comfort.[1]

In such a setting he would have learned the kingly sport of hunting. His own estate in the river city of Chalon would have been equally grandiose, supported by its own productivity but also by taxation and supplemented by tribute from neighboring folk appreciative of the estate's favors. As with other Merovingian kings, his treasury was known to overflow with silver and gold. And this was wealth that in the culture of his times, he was expected to display generously, if not flagrantly.[2]

His reign would become notably prosperous, in imitation of his childhood experience. His father Clothar had maintained and managed in the palace an enormous treasury of gold and jewelry. There too ambassadors and neighboring kings would gather for consultation, energized by opulent feasting on the roasted meats whose delicious aromas filled the vast halls and caverns of the royal household. When Guntram's brother married, the celebration was marked by an entourage of nobles wined and dined with tableware of gold and silver. Laughter and drink merrily filled the halls.[3] By no means did Guntram live simply. And he would see to it that his life's luster would contribute to his productivity, success, and eminence.

SAINT ADELAIDE—ROYAL RETINUE AND REAL ESTATE

As queen, empress, and regent at various stages of her life, Adelaide was one of the most prominent and influential women of her time. Abduction, painful captivity, deaths of children, deaths of two noble husbands, and a daughter-in-law's acrid antipathy also blighted her remarkable life. Despite it all, this beloved and attractive woman was a major credit to her empire. The pride of her citizenry, she reigned with dignity and elegance.

Adelaide had been at home in at least one exquisite Italian castle from the day of her birth. According to the customs of medieval royalty, her parents officially resided in more than one residence. In each location she profited from the attention of maids and other servants. The castles were well protected and enjoyed the spiritual services of resident clergy. Much of

---

1. Boillon, "San Gontranno," para. 1.
2. Wood, *Merovingian Kingdoms*, 65–66, 69.
3. Thierry, *Early Franks*, 7–8, 14.

the property and its lands became hers by gifts from her father, the Frankish King Rudolf II, or later as an inheritance. When her mother Bertha married King Hugh of Italy, he showered them with an exquisite wardrobe and collection of jewels. Later as the wife of his son, King Lothaire, Adelaide became queen of Italy, retaining possession and control of several properties and large productive or recreational tracts of land that Hugh had also given her.

Lothaire had previously gifted her with land as well. Their palace enjoyed the dedication of many servants, including the customary porters, animal keepers, and court physician. A company of musicians enhanced royal relaxation and entertainment. Records, correspondence, and chronicles were in the adept hands of scribes and illuminators. The entire palatial complex was adorned with gold, ivory, and vibrant textiles, while architects and teams of workers contributed to the palace's reconstruction, a project that would enhance the royal image.[4]

When Lothaire died, she inherited his own estates, and she eventually inherited those of her mother. With her marriage to Emperor Otto, her generous dowry consisted of quite expansive French, German, and Slavic territories.[5] The wedding, magnificently celebrated with the great festivity expected of a royal union, brought joy throughout the land.[6] Drawing on resources granted by her new husband, and retaining all the Italian riches that she had previously received,[7] Adelaide was widely notable as quite a wealthy woman. And her fame would grow, due more to her stunning accomplishments than to her conspicuous wealth.

SAINT HOMOBONUS—QUITE COMFORTABLY SITUATED

He complemented his thriving medieval cloth business with avid concern for the poor in his neighborhood. His adoring wife largely assisted him, especially in regard to his social concern. As a successful Italian vendor, Homobonus made his mark on the economic world with her steady though sometimes reluctant support. The couple lived quite comfortably. He enjoyed a substantial inheritance from his father, who had made his fortune

---

4. Golinelli, *Adelaide*, 34–35, 45, 54–55, 103.
5. Wikipedia, "Adelaide of Italy"; Parisse, "Adélaïde de Bourgogne," 14–16.
6. Berrenberg, *Adelheid*, 10; Nash, *Empress Adelheid*, 129, 140.
7. Nash, *Empress Adelheid*, 97–98, 118–19.

as a prosperous tailor and merchandiser.[8] Homobonus shared with his wife an abode reflecting their status. In a newly populated area of Cremona they owned a house,[9] which reflected commercial success but with neither ostentation nor poor taste.[10] Since they were moderately wealthy, they could by twentieth-century standards be called upper-middle class.[11] His holdings were expansive by the standards of his time. Besides the home, he owned some properties outside of Cremona;[12] these included vineyards he had inherited from his father. Here he employed several workers.[13] He was a successful man of his times who knew how to make a fair profit. This, along with his spiritual propensities, would serve him and his city well.

SAINT ELZÉAR OF SABRAN AND BLESSED DELPHINE OF GLANDÈVES—THE YOUNG PICTURE-PERFECT COUPLE AWASH IN SPLENDOR

They had been introduced to one another when both were still in their pre-teens. Both were medieval nobles for whom marriage had been arranged. Having nonetheless found one other quite alluring early on, a few years later Elzéar and Delphine followed their hearts into an amorous marriage but with the unusual agreement that they would permanently abstain from sex. Prized for their virtue as well as their nobility, the youthful couple became endeared to many in the courts of both France and Italy. Their in fact never-consummated marriage was by no means a norm, but in their fourteenth-century culture their deeply affectionate bond provoked sincere admiration among the few who knew of their particular commitment, one affected by spiritual motives.

Their containment of the flesh's sexual urges was no sign however of their indifference to things material or even sensual. The sumptuous surroundings of a French castle welcomed Elzéar's birth. When only twenty-three Elzéar inherited his father's titles, riches, and properties.[14] Delphine's

8. Wikipedia, "Saint Homobonus," para. 3; Wikipedia, "Homobon de Crémone," para. 3.
9. Ricci, "OMOBONO da Cremona," para. 1.
10. Butler, *Lives*, 4:334.
11. Ricci, "Catalogo dei santi," 83.
12. Vauchez, "Saint Homebon," para. 3.
13. Vauchez, *Omobono di Cremona*, 25, 60, 69; Vauchez, "Trafiquant céleste," 119.
14. Butler, *Lives*, 3:661.

inheritance came much earlier when her parents died, leaving her their enormous fortunes and several estates, including one of the province's most majestic castles. In accord with practices of the times, her uncles determined that she be educated in an abbey, not to remove her permanently from her illustrious setting but to prepare her for a lavish life among the nobility. Her eventual marriage to Elzéar thus generated a bond between two of the wealthiest property holders in Provence.

In their first home, Elzéar's inheritance, the luxuries of castle life offered riding in the expansive countryside, raucous hunting, and even highly disciplined training for knighthood. The latter exercises would one day serve Elzéar in successful combat. The couple's early years were marked as well by a relentless current of pleasurable entertainment, festivals, and balls. Elzéar kept quite fit and was an excellent dancer. The couple's life would become somewhat less flamboyant when, a few years later, they moved to Delphine's ancestral home, the palace of her youth, though there would still be the entourage of lords, ladies, and knights mingling amid its halls. The management of the household, with its abundance of household servants and the farmers hired to manage and maintain the couple's vast land holdings, would be marked by extraordinary organization, which we will examine later.

Inheritance and duty brought the couple to a third home in sunny Italy. The surroundings there were as lavish as ever: palatial, elegantly appointed, ennobled by chivalry, and all bathed in Naples' sweet, gently caressing air. Elzéar acquired more manners of courtly life and refined his knightly skills. The court bustled with butlers, servants, valets, caring physicians, and encouraging clergy. Festivities, balls, banquets, theater, and tournaments abounded. The charming and elegant couple fit in splendidly, dazzling the courtly company with their graceful dancing. Elzéar was the picture of knighthood, and Delphine, the image of a finely coiffed fashionable lady.

After Elzéar's untimely death, she inherited his immense fortune. Extensive lands and castles, along with exquisite furnishings, priceless jewelry, and artwork worth a fortune were hers to enjoy. She could literally bask in luxury. But she had other plans.[15]

---

15. Bernard, *Époux vierges*, 15, 19–20, 40, 65, 80, 90, 102, 113–14, 116, 122–24, 161–62.

Contours of Possession—Pleasures of Wealth

SAINT FERDINAND III—RICHES BEYOND COMPARE

The young prince, handsome and athletic, would eventually rule over both the coveted kingdoms of thirteen-century Castile and León, thus attaining great power through their unity. Eventually he would become a majestic and formidable Spanish warrior. His early years in the courts were marked by the fineries of royalty. Upon his mother Berenguela's separation from the King of Leon, his father, Pope Innocent III decreed that Berenguela should hold possession of all her properties, castles, and dowry. In addition, the boy's grandfather, the King of Castile, agreed by treaty with the king of León that Ferdinand would inherit certain other castles. Early on then, Ferdinand found himself ensconced in wealth and routinely surrounded by ladies-in-waiting, chamberlains, knighted guards, and attentive pages. Berenguela's primary castle was an impressive edifice, elegantly studded with parapets. Its patio, which was large enough for soccer, was adorned with decorous Romanesque arches and abloom with flowers of several varieties. A balcony from which Ferdinand later, as king, would preside overlooked a large well-appointed field on which chivalrous contests would be waged. The stately rooms inside were clearly designed to exude grandeur. The walls of great stone could hardly appear cold when complemented by thickly woven tapestries, polished floors whose wood was warmed by plush carpets, and luxuriously trimmed fireplaces whose sparkling fires could illumine all but the farthest reaches of the high ceilings.

Later as an adolescent he was welcomed back to his father's castle in León, a lavish setting where noblemen relished in hunts for boars and bears. Ferdinand's habitual prayerfulness did not deter him from relishing in the lavish festivities of the celebratory royalty. Though habitually attuned to spiritual matters, he assumed the etiquette expected of a proper nobleman. He did not always need to express his devotion in the oratory of the spacious palace. Nor did his piety diminish his enjoyment of leisurely activity, such as riding horseback in the varying conditions of terrain and weather. The seasons spoke to him poetically of grandeur, beauty, and hope. His artistic propensities showed as well when he sang rapturously of romance, chivalry, and heavenly blessings. The royal castle echoed with his melodies while his stepsister Doña Dulce accompanied him on the zither-like psaltery that she strummed with gold and ivory picks.

When he later returned to his mother's castle in Castile, he was welcomed by an entourage of knights, ladies, noble youth, and servants. It was here that he would become King of Castile. At his coronation he wore an elegant tunic—silky white and printed with gold—that rippled over his red leggings and enhanced the gleam of his belt and shoes, all of carved leather and richly inlaid with gold. The purple mantel enhanced his princely radiance. His mother, the Queen, a portrait of elegance, was clad in a full-length blue tunic trimmed with gold and covering a blouse of the finest linen held at her throat by a handsomely crafted brooch. Over her shoulders hung a dark blue mantel studded with stars and glittering of silver.

The wedding of Ferdinand and Beatrice in 1219 was a bright and colorful celebration. Adorned in burgundy velvet and silk-trimmed in gold, the handsome young king approached his bride. She was resplendent in white silk accented with silver as they strode before the joyful congregation overflowing from the castle church. The couple entered the sanctuary where ensued a Mass tastefully embellished with sacred melody. The presiding bishop solemnized the marital union. There followed a lavish, music-filled feast teeming with succulent food and joyful dance. Sportive jousts added to the tumult of fray and excitement.

Ferdinand's sense of proper wardrobe and grooming was reflected even in domestic settings. In evenings at home in the castle, after a day of rough and scuff riding, he would appear in company with well-combed hair and appropriate evening dress. With Beatrice he would frequently enjoy the castle's splendorous meals. His good taste was also reflected in her gleaming pearl necklace. He had in earlier years sent it to her during their engagement.

After his father's death, and upon returning to León as its new king, Ferdinand enjoyed relaxing features of the court. Though usually occupied with administrative duties, he occasionally participated in elaborate rides in the vast forests nearby. Hunters on horseback would utilize dogs and falcons to capture prey; at noontime the party would be treated to formal picnics. Evenings in the castle would come alive with entertainment punctuated by comedians and jesters.[16]

With his later military conquests, Ferdinand found himself amid luxury that exceeded all his previous experience. Particularly impressive was his occupation of Cordoba where the opulent architecture and decor characteristic of the defeated Muslims bedazzled him. Embellishing the palatial realty that was now his were multiple gardens dotted by ponds richly stocked with fish, basins of rippling quicksilver, gold and marble roofs and

---

16. Fernández, *King of Castile*, 2, 17, 19, 22–24, 29, 31, 41, 62, 64, 68–49, 123–24, 173, 189.

walls, ivory arches decked with ebony and precious stones, and pillars of marble and crystal.[17]

Lavish was not a word strong enough to predicate the lifelong surroundings that Ferdinand enjoyed. He was a royal gentleman who lived in splendor and, by his astounding quests, carved an unforgettable and perhaps unmatchable niche in history.

SAINT MARGARET OF SCOTLAND— A LADY OF REFINED TASTES

The young English lady's ship had been swept off course by tumultuous winds and was beached on the shores of Scotland. Not long thereafter, by fortuitous circumstances, she married the country's king, with whom she as queen eventually had many children. Born into English royalty and exiled in eleventh-century Hungary, Margaret became accustomed to wealth from an early age. The proverbial silver spoon was part of her little-girl fare. Later on, as an adolescent back in England, she and her family enjoyed aristocratic privileges of protection, housing, servants, and education. Moreover, her father Edward had brought many luxury items, including finery of gold and silver, from the royal court in Hungary.[18] Lavish possessions were as normal to Margaret as her island nation's fog and mist. Her fortune included a very large inheritance from her royal English forebears, most of which she had with her on first arriving in Scotland. To her marriage she brought a large dowry that more than amply accorded with her status. Her funds thereafter became further enhanced by an accumulation of local rents and taxes, income that was impressively sizeable. Her husband Malcolm was wealthy as well, enjoying the assets of Scottish properties and English revues. The aristocracy of which they were a privileged part glowed of gold and silver.

The scene of her marriage to Malcolm was Dunfermline Palace, set in thick, resplendent woods and known to later ages for its majestic Gothic walls, soaring turret, and ornate tapestries. She moved into a lap of luxury. But in those initial days of Malcolm and Margaret's residence, the royal Scottish dwellings were somewhat drab by English tastes, the ones to which the younger Margaret had become accustomed. The setting was rich in form and foliage, but overall rather dark, and perhaps brooding, awaiting

17. Fitzhenry, *Saint Fernando III*, 16, 102–4, 106, 226.
18. Nagy, *St. Margaret*, 16.

a welcome transformation. The robust Scots had been accustomed to the noble but stark features of their architecture and decor.

King Malcolm, who had earlier made his own mark on the palace's architecture, appreciated what was royal luxury by Scottish standards of the times. He was a wealthy monarch, evidenced by an extensive luxurious wardrobe and a large collection of wares crafted in precious metals. His palace was apparently an impressive timbered structure with its own chapel and flanked by a kitchen, a stable, various workshops, and quarters for servants and guards. Inside was stately and rugged oak furniture and an abundance of wine, local produce, and Scottish fare.

Yet Margaret enhanced the routines, furnishings, and chambers considerably, evoking a remarkable transformation of the palace and the court, especially through the finery and dress of the attendant knights and ladies, whose numbers and rank she notably increased and whom she managed with aplomb. She also brightened the king's wardrobe. For herself she chose the splendid gowns of delicate, brightly shimmering wool adorned with various precious stones. In winter her long, flowing cloak was secured at the top with a lovely gold fastener.

She also brought to the royal environment luxurious trappings and the luster of precious metals. Attractive furnishings in a wide variety of colors brightened former drabness. Formal meals served on platters of silver and gold became a standard feature.[19] Margaret's taste for the lavish was replicated when the royal dwelling was later moved to Edinburgh.[20] For she understood how such embellishments could contribute to the glamour and prestige of the court, and even to the reputation of Scotland itself. With these embellishments was bound even the Scottish court's heightened authority.[21] Indeed all of Scottish nobility was brought to a new level of refinement. By this expanded network of social and commercial interaction, even the prosperity of the citizenry generally was heightened. It was as if the abundance of the royal palace was a fountain overflowing to the rest of the kingdom and nurturing its economic growth.

Shortly after her marriage to the king, she employed her citizen-servants to build a chapel on the palace grounds. She embellished it with ornamentation of gold, silver, and precious gems.[22] Amid the decor was a

19. Marshall, "Malcolm Canmore," para. 14.
20. Dunlop, *Queen Margaret of Scotland*, 25–26, 46–48, 50, 64–65.
21. Turgot, *Vita Margaretae*, 152, 164.
22. Keene, *Saint Margaret*, 37, 42, 61.

very expensive, richly adorned cross. In naming the beautiful church after the Holy Trinity, her desire was to ensure her own spiritual enrichment, the growing faith of her husband, and the enduring virtue of her future children, whom she assumed would also enjoy prosperity.[23] Margaret's Bibles and devotional books were adorned by a smith with silver, gold, and jewels. This artistry was done at the behest of her husband, King Malcolm, who could not read but greatly appreciated Margaret's dedication to reading such texts to him. She lived in splendor. But what rendered her eminently historical was the wealth of talents and achievements that marked her reign.

SAINT LOUIS IX—THE EPITOME OF ROYAL LUXURY

Crowned king of France as a mere tween, the impressive nobleman attained prominence in his domain as a well-educated and astute ruler. Until he could assume the throne on his own, his mother Blanche efficiently ruled the kingdom and brought it international fame. As king, Louis treasured the love of his dear wife Marguerite. The royal castle of the young king and queen was at Pontoise. Their lands and household were copiously appointed and at great expense. The royal household buzzed with squires, smiths, stable-boys, cooks, pages, bakers, pantry servants, a cart driver, a butler, ushers, clerks, and runners. In sum, there were some sixty specially trained servants, plus a chaplain. This impressive entourage was complemented by some thirty men-at-arms who likely served as the king's bodyguards. Festivities such as those in honor of newly dubbed knights were celebrated with magnificent flair.[24]

Besides attending to his own needs and those of his family, Louis loved to entertain guests at meals. He wined and dined the wealthy in accord with their thirteenth-century expectations. As an avid reader he particularly welcomed discussions with experts on substantive topics.[25] Prominent nobility had to be suitably honored as well and were duly impressed by his generous hospitality. The table was copious and the preparations extensive. Spices were stored in hand-crafted silver receptacles. By the king's command the fare would be exemplary: an abundance of wine, entrees, cheeses, fruits, and desserts for the swarms of guests.

23. Turgot, *Dunfermline Vita*, 172, 178–79.
24. Butler, *Lives*, 3:395.
25. Folz, *Saints roi*, 108.

Tailors summoned to ply their skills in accord with norms of fashion carefully observed rules applying to the various levels of prestige in the court. Though in general Louis preferred simpler attire, he dressed royally for special occasions. His wardrobe thus featured silk, satin, ermine and sable. No doubt Marguerite complemented and enhanced his demeanor and attire.

Outside the castle, the king relished in his menagerie, where exotic animals such as lions could draw his attention or entertain his interests. As to royal outdoorsmanship, his retinue was well equipped for the sport of hunting, though he seems to have not enjoyed it so much personally. As befitted nobility however, he kept an entourage of horses, dogs, falcons, and hawks suitable for those who enjoyed the sport. The collection of horses far exceeded the number needed for hunting; for the king also provided them as mounts for his approximately thirty knights and as gifts to many of his associates.[26]

The king and his lovely queen thus lived well, if not in splendor. They had multiple residences acquired at different times during Louis's reign. Since he traveled widely to stay in contact with his people and to go on pilgrimages, he enjoyed all of his domiciles, and with regularity. His palace in Paris was a three-story fortress-like edifice equipped with a tower and encompassing—besides sumptuous living quarters—a garden, an archive, a library, and Sainte-Chapelle, a magnificent Gothic church that would eventually become world-renowned as an architectural gem.[27] The king and queen hardly retreated from luxury. But in the context of splendor, Louis made exemplary gains for France's populace and the royal couple's beloved church.

VENERABLE PIERRE TOUSSAINT— ENRICHED IN MANY WAYS

Having been born into a family of well treated and highly regarded domestic slaves, Pierre's kind master brought him from the island of St. Domingue, now Haiti, to live in late eighteenth-century New York. There he entered the lucrative hairdressing profession. Serving the needs of polite society, mostly French-American, he eventually became a widely known financial success. Though for decades a slave, a luxurious lifestyle was not new to

---

26. Richard, *St. Louis*, 64, 81–82.
27. Le Goff, *Saint Louis*, 426–27, 430–33, 514–16, 562.

him. As a boy he was quite accustomed to the luxury of the St. Domingan plantation mansion and the splendor of its appointments, many of them exquisite products of French artistry.

The four-story house readied in New York for him and his master's family was, with its garden and patio in the back, spacious enough to include servant quarters. The new home was stylishly furnished and provided a welcoming atmosphere for him and the other slaves to experience the social life and merriment of the household. His hairdressing trade eventually became so successful that he was later able to provide his master's widow—who sadly had become bankrupt—with a weekly stipend. He even provided her with some luxuries that added to her status among her peers. Over the years, as his assets multiplied, one of New York's affluent senior citizens called him the richest man she knew.[28]

Eventually he became quite comfortably self-sufficient. Having initially lived in a comfortable apartment, he and his wife Juliette subsequently moved into a large house, pleasantly and tastefully furnished, where parties and other gatherings transpired in an atmosphere of gentility. Dinners aglow with fine linen and silver reflected touches of Parisian refinement. The house was large enough to have a separate apartment for their adopted niece's tutor, to accommodate a gentlemanly border, and to provide a home for Juliette's mother. The couple routinely enjoyed their wealth, even as they shared it with the destitute.[29]

In their later years the pair purchased a house that was a few blocks away; it was smaller but of equal elegance.[30] Juliette tastefully appointed it with the exquisite furniture brought from France, while through the fine-laced curtains gentle light brought sheen and shimmer to the silver and china. Besides loving to host fashionable gatherings, the two also relished entertainment, regularly attending plays, operas, and concerts. When the circus was in town, Pierre and Juliette were sure to treat their beloved niece to its amusements.[31] Here was a man and lovely wife—a couple that enjoyed good company, were toasts of the town, and were admired benefactors. Their fame would over the years become uncommonly widespread.

---

28. Hanley, "Pierre Toussaint," para. 88.
29. Lee, *Memoir of Pierre Toussaint*, 14–15, 48, 55, 82, 99–100.
30. Sheehan and Odell, *Pierre Toussaint*, 165, 219.
31. Jones, *Pierre Toussaint*, 105, 184.

Good and Wealthy

BLESSED FRÉDÉRIC OZANAM—A KEEN SENSE OF THE PLEASURABLE

His early interests in religion, social issues, and literature led him to acquire advanced university decrees and to gain widespread prominence as one of France's most eminent intellectuals. Never satisfied with thought alone, whether regarding religion or social action, the distinguished Professor Ozanam engaged in hands-on and personable assistance to those in physical or emotional need. Through his efforts, the Society of St. Vincent de Paul became an immense charitable institution with chapters worldwide. Yet this warmhearted and rather unassuming scholar was hardly averse to taking pleasure in some of life's generous offerings.

Frédéric was born into a nineteenth-century family that was quite comfortably middle class, enjoying income from his father's medical practice and publications. When he was a teen, Frédéric traveled with his parents on an extended trip to Italy. The family visited relatives there while his younger brother seems to have been left in the care of a trusted servant. She had become a major caretaker of Frédéric when his older sister passed away, and by the time of his mother's death nineteen year later, she was assisted by at least one other servant. For Frédéric, later leaving home meant no drastic change in economic status. By the age of twenty-six he was earning a substantial and reliable income by an endowed teaching position he had assumed in Lyon.

While practicing law there he was able to vacation in Paris. Later he and his wife Amélie celebrated their honeymoon in Italy. The trip, which Frédéric called enchanting, included memorable visits to historical sites in Sicily and was crowned by ten days in Rome. There they enjoyed a private papal audience, which the pope wished to be more of a friendly chat than a mannerly formality.[32] As a notable professor, and leader of his now international charitable society, Frédéric was also famed for several Italian translations of his work on Dante. Appreciative of whatever royalties the book might generate, he encouraged recognition of it. Somewhat later he and Amélie traveled to Italy again and were able to enjoy the country's countless historic, artistic, and religious attractions at a leisurely pace. The six-month trip of 1847 afforded Frédéric some much needed rest because of his waning health. Amélie, the little daughter Marie, and the family's maid went with him. Comforted by relaxation, he nonetheless found time for research

---

32. Slattery, *Blessed Frederic Ozanan*, 6–8; Baunard, *His Correspondence*, 187.

and the pleasures of such centers as Florence, Rome, Assisi, and Venice,[33] as he laid the groundwork for later publications with Italian themes.

The couple's comfortable Parisian apartment offered a splendid view of the city's decorous Luxembourg Gardens. Initially there was only one domestic servant for a household where contentment reigned. She had been in the employ of the Ozanam family since her youth, well before Frédéric's birth, and in the newlyweds' household, she served with firm devotion. Her counsel was warmly respected, like that of a grandmother recalling noble family traditions. While Frédéric worked at his desk, Amélie often provided pleasant music at the piano they had acquired at considerable cost. The atmosphere of the apartment was further enlivened by regular meals for relatives, friends, or professional associates. Not that Frédéric was keen on finery and formalities. He was uncomfortable amid a pretentious display of wealth. Yet Amélie early on had suggested that his professional life could reasonably profit by his spending more on his clothing and by broadening his social circle. It was an apt recommendation, for he was somewhat fashion conscious[34] and valued friendship enormously. Eventually, with the help of two domestic servants, Amélie flawlessly and with gracious mirth orchestrated the generous Ozanam hospitality.[35]

Frédéric tended to be a bit frugal but instinctively knew how to allow himself and his family an enchanting trip now and then.[36] In their earlier years the family's summer home outside of Paris serenely overlooked a river valley and offered comforting occasional respite. Later on at a country home, also outside the French capital, a petite and peaceful garden became a place of rest and renewal for the family and its guests.[37] Before the birth of their daughter, Amélie in turn allowed herself occasional refreshing trips to the French coast when Frédéric was away.[38] During his final days he enjoyed Amélie's comfort and the adulation of local admirers near his Italian villa.[39] With his generous disposition, he was a man who unpretentiously enjoyed many of life's comforts and pleasures. In such a context he

---

33. Bernardelli, *Storia*, 80–81, 84–93.
34. Ozanam, *Letters*, 37, 178, 189, 224.
35. Cholvy, *Christianisme a besoin*, 13, 140–43, 145–47, 207, 210.
36. Sickinger, *Antoine Frédéric Ozanam*, 8, 10, 19, 26, 103–4.
37. O'Meara, *Frédéric Ozanam*, 233–34, 243–44, 344.
38. Harrison, *Romantic Catholics*, 211, 216.
39. Scott, "Frédéric Ozanam," 49–50.

succeeded in articulating an impressive social vision and in putting it into practice in a manner that endures to this day.

BLESSED VICTOIRE RASOAMANARIVO—CULTURED TASTE AND PROPER REFINEMENT

From her youth Victoire was highly esteemed by the royalty of her nation. Having converted from her native religion as a teen, she professed her Christian faith and became one of its greatest champions during a time of religious discrimination. The survival of Christianity in its multiple denominations was due to her intrepid leadership.

She was born into a nineteenth-century Malagasy family counted among the wealthiest and most influential on the island today called Madagascar. Raised in one of the impressive mansions near the royal palace, this young black native could have been easily spoiled by her leisurely and carefree childhood. A household slave served with dutiful dedication as her private nurse. By the age of seven she was free to circulate at lavish banquets in a grand hall where the queen served as many as two hundred dignitaries, including white Europeans. The court and attendees, elegantly dressed à l'européene, danced to music resonant of international motifs.[40]

As a young lady she donned the elegant finery of courtly dress and manners that imitated expensive Victorian fashion. She adopted the frills but not the pretension exhibited by some of her distinguished peers. Marriage soon brought her an immense fortune and a sumptuous household of her own—riches that she clearly enjoyed.[41] Well over three hundred slaves were at her beck and call, thirty of whom attended to the palatial home designed by her husband to reflect the finest advancements of current architecture. Decorous tiles elegantly adorned the edifice's exterior walls, which faced a lovely garden. A colonnade gave way to a beautiful veranda hugging the facade. Inside, the main corridor was adorned by a central staircase. Artistically crafted windows brought variegated light to the rosewood furnishings that were selectively embellished with bas-relief. Copper-gilded chairs that Victoire found particularly attractive brightly dotted the chambers. Outside and beyond the garden stretched the lucrative slave-managed field.

---

40. Ramahery, *Ange visible*, 41.
41. Molinari, *Summarium super miracolo*, 31.

Yet, even as a woman of stature and prominent member of the court, Victoire's generous nature and sense of personal duty were scarcely attenuated by such amenities. On the contrary, her lavish surroundings provided a salubrious setting for spirituality and charity. Officers of the military helped her find in the realm hardship cases to which she could give her heartfelt attention. She often invited the poor and her household slaves to meals in the majestic dining room.[42] In her final days of deteriorating health, she arranged for her noble surroundings to be decorated for solemnity, hallowed by choral music, and adorned with an entourage of reverent slaves providing what she believed was a context befitting the dignity of the Sacrament that she prayerfully received.[43] Victoire's luxury framed a heart of gold. And Madagascar could enduringly take pride in much more than her fame and status.

SAINTS LOUIS AND MARIE-AZÉLIE MARTIN— A PROSPEROUS, ENTERPRISING COUPLE

The Martins were successful business partners in nineteenth-century France. Louis, gifted in artistry and design, sold a profitable watchmaking concern in order to engage in his wife Zélie's internationally renowned lacemaking business. Their joyous household of five devoted daughters was in later years saddened by Zélie's death. The widowed father carried on dutifully, efficiently, and lovingly as a single parent. The new setting continued to be nurturing and genuinely agreeable.

Louis had been born into a respected French military family. His father was a captain in Napoleon's army. Louis' familiarity with rather comfortable living endured into adulthood as his watchmaking and jewelry business in Alençon flourished. After his marriage and several children, customers were coming to him in growing numbers. Meantime his wife Zélie was having great success at her own enterprise. By the time of their wedding both were quite stable financially because of property holdings and investments. They lived in patent comfort but without extravagance in quarters large enough to accommodate them, their two businesses, and Louis's parents. Zélie's business expanded to such a degree in France's growing economy that Louis averred astutely that he should partner with her in the venture.

---

42. Fourcadier, *Vie héroïque*, 9, 23, 53–54.

43. Marie, "August 8, 2008," para. 20; Simon-Perret, *Victoire Rasoamanarivo*, 19, 53–54, 58, 63–64, 66, 144.

Good and Wealthy

Though they did not live opulently, by their trade they were nonetheless relatively prosperous, if not rather wealthy. Zélie continued to work outside the home even after Louis entered her business, not to amass a great fortune but to successfully establish suitable dowries for their daughters.[44] Moreover, the Martins enjoyed seeing their children well dressed, and their household was stylishly furnished. The children had an abundance of toys,[45] the household enjoyed domestic services, and Louis's love of travel and adventure awakened their enthusiasm for France's multiple natural wonders.[46]

Having been bereaved of his wife, Louis moved his remaining family, all daughters, to Lisieux. There he could enjoy retirement, though he still had to administer his assets. He and Zélie had built up quite a fortune in their trades. Louis's large number of investments and his extensive real estate holdings allowed him to retire comfortably at an untypically early age.[47] His brother-in-law found the family a very attractive and quite large four-bedroom house set in artfully landscaped gardens. Louis tastefully outfitted the cozy rooms with carved oak and elegant walnut furnishings. On the living-room mantel presided gracefully a Martin clock, a cherished elegant memento of times past. Plush drapery complemented the parquet floors, while artwork adorned the walls. Louis devoted himself to maintaining the home's beautiful garden.

Though the girls had regular household chores, and though Louis encouraged studiousness in their schooling, there was ample recreational time. Several vacations typically breathed of seaside breezes enlivening a house rented for one or two months.[48] The family enjoyed times for theater and for trips to Paris and Rome.[49] Once Louis himself, though missing terribly his daughters who were in the care of their aunt, made a trip from Lisieux to Paris, Munich, Bavaria, Vienna, Constantinople, Athens, Milan, and Rome.[50] Thus, even though the life he adopted in Lisieux was simpler than what he had enjoyed for many years in Alençon, he could later be noted by a Vatican historical document as a saint who overall continued to

---

44. Cadéot, *Zélie Martin*, 30–31, 55, 62.
45. Louis Martin and Zélie Martin, *Deeper Love*, 27.
46. Wikipedia, "Louis Martin and Marie-Azélie Guérin," para. 7.
47. Renda, introduction to *Deeper Love*, xxvii.
48. Piat, *Story of a Family*, 41, 67–68, 141, 267, 285, 292–93.
49. Di Nicola and Danese, *Amore scritto in cielo*, 160–61.
50. Louis Wust and Marjorie Wust, *Louis Martin*, 77, 119, 200, 240–45.

enjoy relative prosperity.[51] Zélie would have shared to the full extent in such delight had she lived long enough to be with him and their daughters in his final days. Even with her fewer years however, the sum of the couple's lives would be edifying and historical.

SAINT GIANNA BERETTA MOLLA— ENJOYING FAMILIAL DELIGHTS

Every workday Gianna's father commuted by train to Milan from his family's home. He provided generously for them, ensuring that they were fairly well off, though they enjoyed their comfort unobtrusively.[52] The children learned from their parents to live cheerily but simply.[53] Though not opulent, the Berretas' twentieth-century house in Bergamo was large enough for a couple with eight children, and it had a fine garden where the youngsters could enjoy the outdoors. Among the entertainments the family enjoyed were classical music concerts and operas.

Later, when living near Genoa as the bombings of World War I began, the family was able to take refuge in their summer mountain home close to Switzerland. Nonetheless, Gianna's upbringing was rather unpretentious. When later studying medicine, she did not forbear the enjoyment of theater and fine clothing. Subsequently as a medical professional she was intent on budgeting for operas, paintings, fashion magazines, and a reservedly elegant but perfectly stylish wardrobe suitable for any given occasion. During her initial years as a physician in Mesero, she drove a modest Fiat 500.

Her future husband Pietro Molla gave her, besides an engagement ring that she called magnificent, a gold watch and a pearly necklace as signs of his love. For their honeymoon she and Pietro joyfully traveled to nearly a dozen famed and exotic locations in Italy, including Rome and Capri. Soon afterwards Gianna was able to accompany Pietro on business trips to Germany, Holland, England, Denmark, and Sweden.

They then settled outside of Magenta in a two-story house surrounded by land beautifully dotted with flowers and shade trees. Summers brought serenity, recreation, and rejuvenation after a two-hour drive to Courmayeur, the Alpine resort town in northwestern Italy. The couple's home in Mesero reflected Gianna's penchant for practical elegance. Professional photos

---

51. Ziegler, "History awaits."
52. Guerriero, introduction to *Journey of Our Love*, 5.
53. Brown, *No Greater Love*, 4.

with silver frames glistened in the rooms. Pietro's study bulged with books. Gianna's office in the city was tastefully appointed.

After the birth of their first child, she and Pietro were able to afford a housekeeper,[54] a truly devoted young woman who remained faithful to the family for many years.[55] Gianna and Pietro further enjoyed traveling throughout Europe. Together they also enjoyed theater, concerts, party-going, and dancing.

Until their engagement Pietro was, by his own admission, something of a workaholic. Convinced that he needed more leisure and fun, Gianna saw to it that they had season tickets to plays and concerts.[56] A favorite pastime of hers was mountain climbing and skiing in the exquisite vistas of the Alps.[57] As the family grew, getaways for all became a must. The children particularly delighted in the colors and light of their vacation home. Some who observed the Molla lifestyle commented sarcastically that Gianna and her family could enjoy such pleasures because "they have money and means."[58] But those observers did not know the Mollas' whole story.

BLESSEDS LUIGI AND MARIA BELTRAME QUATTROCCHI—RICH IN FAMILY LIFE

Here was a young talented couple, a highly educated woman and man whose warm personal qualities shone in abundance. These nurtured the Italian pair's remarkably profound mutual love, led them to establish an exemplary family, induced heroic decision in facing a problematic pregnancy, and animated their widespread public service. Luigi grew up in the care of his comfortably middle class adoptive parents. Maria was raised in a military family that was further distinguished by a noble heritage.

For some years after their marriage in 1905 the couple resided in Rome with Maria's parents and grandparents; the household was staffed by dedicated servants. This remained the Beltrame Quattrocchi family home even after the passing of the two older generations. It was a bright and spacious eight-room apartment whose third-floor balconies gave splendid views of a historic piazza and elegant governmental buildings. The home's

---

54. Wallace and Jablonski, *Saint Gianna*, 7, 27, 57.
55. Pelucchi, *Saint Gianna*, 7–8, 46, 68, 72, 74, 77.
56. Molla and Guerriero, *Saint Gianna Molla*, 58, 68.
57. Pastoral Centre, "Life of St. Gianna Beretta Molla," para. 14.
58. Da Riese Pio X, *Love of Life*, 37, 125–29, 131, 146, 165–66.

cozy rooms, glistening with story-telling stained-glass windows, were exquisitely appointed, though not opulently, and reflective of Maria's refined Florentine taste. While Maria was engaged in writing professionally, a competent staff supported her motherly and wifely attention to the household and family. Luigi did so too, firmly committed to sharing with his wife what he regarded as the momentous role of a parent.

For respite and fun, the family vacationed variously. They had a beautiful home with a fine ocean view on a popular Mediterranean seacoast several miles south of Rome. This was a spot particularly favored at Easter time when the children were young. It left them with pleasant memories of adventuresome boating and fishing. Later on the family would center its vacation activities on a mountain home rented for entire summers. Maria relished the clear, splendorous peaks decidedly more than the salt air of the seaside. When the couple had only one child left in the nest, Luigi built a getaway home on a parcel of scenic mountain land.[59] Attractively constructed of stone framed by wrought iron and wood, the house was simply but quite tastefully furnished under Maria's guiding hand. The abode's natural setting was exquisite, amiably offering marvelous colorful vistas. Maria scarcely thought that enjoying the picturesque surroundings was undue indulgence; rather, she regarded such contentment as an appropriate opportunity for the family's renewal.[60] Getaways there were always punctuated by relaxation, reading, extended conversations, vigorous hiking, and an untiring enjoyment of nature's wonders.

Moreover, the couple frequently enjoyed theater, concerts, and operas.[61] Maria did not believe that striving for sanctity necessarily involved the renunciation of wealth, though she and Luigi intentionally avoided what they thought was superfluous.[62] He felt that everything in one's home should be procured to bring joy. Yet to him the work that brought financial gain was, second only to spiritual enrichment, of significant value for the dignity it expressed and the opportunity it offered for self-improvement through expending one's innate talents.[63]

Living through two world wars, the Beltrame Quattrocchis occasionally faced periods of financial stress but met them with confidence and

---

59. Savior.org, "Blessed Luigi Beltrame Quattrocchi," paras. 8, 11.
60. Beltrame Quattrocchi, *Ordito e la trama*, 8.
61. Beltrame Quattrocchi, *Lui, lei, noi, loro*, 16, 28, 40–41, 43–44.
62. Papàsogli, *Quesi borghesi*, 42, 71, 181–82, 340.
63. Beltrame Quattrocchi, *Lui, lei, noi, loro*, 7.

hope.[64] With their otherwise considerable resources they heartily responded to seemingly endless appeals for assistance or support.[65] The couple's compassion and even courage in such situations evoked, as we will see, much admiration.

---

64. O'Neel, *Thirty-Nine New Saints*, 131, 133.
65. Marie, "April 8, 2008," para. 13.

CHAPTER 3

Making the Most of Things— Tenets and Tactics

WE ARE PROBING THE colorful histories of saintly women and men who enjoyed the trappings of wealth and whose lifestyles might in some cases even be called flamboyant. For many of them, with wealth came power and other manifestations of eminence in the material world. Inordinate attachment to material things, or extravagant basking in comfortable circumstances, can forestall sound judgment and thus encumber either prudent, gainful management of affairs or fair and edifying treatment of others, particularly subordinates or society's less fortunate. Yet such impairments hardly characterized the demeanor of the kindly personalities we are considering here. On the contrary, they exerted favorable, if not praiseworthy, oversight that yielded gain, not only in areas of finance and commerce but widely as well in the domain of social interaction. They lived with wealth and power in ways that were both moderate and estimable. We view them now from these perspectives.

SAINT GUNTRAM—ANGER TAMED AND REFINED

Here was a reprehensible young nobleman who in time became a respectable ruler—the prominent king who had reveled in the sumptuous court of sixth-century Burgundy, with its refined society and fine wine. Here was Guntram, who learned to manage and tame his deeply embedded tendency toward vicious and violent reaction to perceived attack. He could indeed draw more effectively on his more angelic side. By an easygoing approach he could exhibit a pacifying mildness of manner, if not an efficient indifference. Some challenges need gentle management; others solve themselves if left alone.

Typically energized by such dispositions, he could, when offended or attacked, display gentle clemency, forgiving even those who attempted to assassinate him. Once when he recognized that he had unjustly ordered an execution, he repented. As to the incessant propensity of his contemporaries toward party- or culture-driven disputes and wars, he remained aloof, not allowing himself to be affected, or allowing certain outcomes of a dispute to redound to his benefit. What once appeared as youthful lethargy emerged in his maturity as resourceful equanimity. He thus appeared as the ideal leader who modeled virtue while embroiled in a culture of incivility and corruption.[1]

When he engaged in battle, it was nearly always defensive. War to him seemed a merely tolerable though sometimes necessary disturbance of the tranquility so dear to him by his acquired temperament.[2] His aggression was limited to engagement against the barbarian Goths, whom he apparently regarded as heretics. He strictly ordered his army to fight fairly in conformity with rules of justice and particularly to refrain from pillaging religious institutions and their personnel. Any booty was to be donated to the poor and the church.[3] Guntram's commitment to demonstrating strength with a minimum of necessary violence served him and his kingdom well.

SAINT ADELAIDE—SHREWD DIPLOMAT AND PRODUCTIVE MANAGER

She had ruled over grateful and admiring citizenries in various ways—as queen, as empress, and as regent. Despite multiple setbacks and sorrows, this gorgeous woman assumed responsibilities with dignity and carried them out with outstanding competence and efficacy.

Adelaide was a highly cultured and educated woman who spoke four languages. They would serve her well as she seemed to bound from country to country in varied positions of authority. From her youth multiple royal attendants would have educated her in French, German, Latin, and Italian. She would have heard the reports and requests of the empire's numerous

---

1. Heinzelmann, *Gregory of Tours*, 51–57.
2. Thierry, *Early Franks*, 147.
3. Grégoire de Tours, "Histoire des Francs," paras. 36–37.

Making the Most of Things—Tenets and Tactics

nobles and ambassadors that frequented her father's tenth-century palace in France.[4] This was surely an environment conducive to the development of her competencies. Thus in later years on a royal throne in another country—namely, as King Lothaire's queen in Italy—she lost no time in clearly displaying the qualities of a gifted ruler.[5]

After Lothaire's untimely death, her dramatic meeting with Emperor Otto I was followed by her marriage to him. She encouraged her new husband to improve his ability to read and write. With her appreciation of learning and social grace, she considerably enhanced the cultural life of the German court. Accompanying her inherent wisdom was her prudence in seeking the counsel of several revered and accomplished clerics.[6] Wielding much power within the palace, she would have typically overseen its highest ranking officers, including the treasurer. Her management of the entire imperial complex, its operations, and its activities was quite astute. She would have been assisted by her own corps of secretaries and supported by her own team of chaplains.

She was also attentive to needs outside the palace. While honoring many a needy person with outright financial assistance, she frequently offered benefactions to help someone's poverty turn into wealth. Her political influence would have been evident by her managing the allotment of gifts in forging alliances. As the emperor's partner, Empress Adelaide's influence, both in the country and in the imperial family, were essential to maintaining political order. This was especially important and evident when the emperor was away. He clearly trusted her to represent or assist him in political matters and in decisions where imperial influence was significant in ecclesiastical circles. She provided major assistance to Abbot Majolus of the Cluny monastery during the historical Cluniac reform of the European church. Monastic renewal would stimulate refreshed religious practice throughout the continent and reinvigorate service of the poor.

From the earliest days of her marriage to Otto, Adelaide began her frequent custom of accompanying him on his extensive missions and imperial visitations, not just as his companion but as a partner in governance.[7] This was especially the case when their children had grown older.[8]

4. Golinelli, *Adelaide*, 35–36.
5. Nash, *Empress Adelheid*, 141.
6. Butler, *Lives*, 4:573.
7. Bäumer, *Otto und Adelheid*, 38–39, 67–68, 74, 87; Nash, *Empress Adelheid*, 133, 142.
8. Parisse, "Adélaïde de Bourgogne," 17.

Her role of imperial administrator was enhanced and even fell to her exclusively as she demonstrated her power as quasi-occupant and even protector of the throne.[9] Otto I had died years earlier. With the death of their son, Otto II, she began a tenure as the regent for her grandson Otto III. She was an extremely wise administrator and exercised extraordinary influence in both Italy and Germany.[10] While the enemies of the empire were many, she never took revenge on them.[11] Not only that, in many cases she gave help and support as repayment for injury.[12] By the plan she marshaled, she creatively demonstrated how foes could become allies.

SAINT HOMOBONUS—ENERGETIC AND CRAFTY

Vending cloth and attending to the nearby needy were enough to keep him busy most of his days. In such enterprises this robust Italian gentleman was happily accompanied by a supportive wife. As a prosperous twelfth-century businessman Homobonus conjoined his desire for profit with a strong penchant for philanthropy. His wife assisted him in professional and charitable interests, except when in her view they unduly interfered with normal family life. In his day he was a popular and beloved figure in both the medieval worlds of business and politics. A master of his trade,[13] he worked hard in the company he had streamlined to facilitate his industriousness.[14] He expended much physical effort—probably with less stress than by those not of his large size—especially at market time when he had to set up and display his wares. The wool trade was in that era a vibrant and highly competitive industry. The product was in great demand on the market.[15]

Quite the entrepreneur, he traveled far and wide, even overseas at times, to promote his company[16] and to serve as a money changer.[17] As a businessman he was scrupulously honest. Though it was a turbulent time,

---

9. Gilsdorf, introduction to *Queenship*, 9–12.
10. Wikipedia, "Adelaide di Borgogna (Imperatrice)"; Nash, *Empress Adelheid*, 147–49.
11. Campbell, "St. Adelaide."
12. Odilo of Cluny, *Epitaph*, 132, 134.
13. Vauchez, *Laity*, 59.
14. Butler, *Lives*, 4:334.
15. Bonometti, "L'iconografia dimezzata," 23.
16. Ricci, "OMOBONO da Cremona," para. 2.
17. Vauchez, "Trafiquant céleste," 118.

when Italian cities were seeking independence, he succeeded in amassing a considerable fortune in his hometown, Cremona. The city's economy was enriched by his profitable merchandising, particularly in the wool trade. The large proportion of his profits that he gave as a benefactor of the poor would mark him today as a notable philanthropist.[18]

In the political realm he used his influence to minimize violence between contending factions. He built bridges of peace between dissenting parties. There were heated political and ecclesiastical disputes in his region of Lombardy; differing parties of church and state vied for power and superiority. The region was victimizing itself by a nearly suicidal civil war, a kind of class warfare with the middle class at odds with the aristocrats.[19] But Homobonus remained always the helpful arbiter rather than a partisan. At one point he literally brought words of benevolence and accord to two armed factions. And, except to bind wounds and bury the dead, that was the end of their war.[20] Thus in trying diligently to serve his city's interests, he exhibited the kind of devoted support that in the view of his contemporaries was comparable to participating in a Crusade.[21] His talent, diligence, and kindly disposition would not soon be forgotten.

SAINT ELZÉAR OF SABRAN AND BLESSED DELPHINE OF GLANDÈVES—ADROIT MANAGERS

Noble estates of France had been their home. Royal trappings of Italy became their inheritance. Elzéar and Delphine were young, exciting, and beautiful—he, fulfilling images of knightly chivalry, she, embodying the elegance of an enchanting and refined young Lady. Though bonded by impassioned love and committed to one another by lifelong marriage, this endearing couple chose to forego any sexual contact. Lying together in bed meant enjoying heartfelt intimacy by mere proximity while fully clothed. Such uncommon detachment from sensuality by no means signaled that they were immune from ardent affection or from discriminating sensitivity to life's material benefits. Privileged by their nobility, they were immersed in the finery and elegance of fourteenth-century courtly life. And they demonstrated appropriate authority and leadership in such settings.

18. Wikipedia, "Saint Homobonus," para. 4; Vauchez, "Trafiquant céleste," 120.
19. Ricci, "OMOBONO da Cremona," para. 3.
20. Pedretti, *Sant' Omobono*, 25, 36–39.
21. Vauchez, *Omobono*, 21.

Good and Wealthy

Elzéar masterfully managed the second household of his marriage with Delphine. It was the palace of her childhood; there he warmly demanded diligence of the domestic workers yet clearly appreciated their benevolence. The devout Delphine shared this role with him, wisely realizing that her dignity as a wife required that she behave more like an efficient partner than a reclusive nun. Growing up in an abbey, she deeply appreciated contemplative monastic life. But she also learned there the skills necessary to maintain and supervise an orderly household. Among inhabitants of the abbey, begging was not a custom. The nuns there enjoyed being resourceful and self-sufficient, though welcoming what gifts might come from the outside. Such an upbringing left its mark on Delphine. She had previously shared with Elzéar the effectual management of their first home, the one to which she would later return when he was temporarily called away. He left with great confidence in her executive competencies.[22]

At the age of twenty-three Elzéar traveled to Italy in order to claim his recently inherited lordship at Ariano. He was so ill-received by his noble subordinates in nearby Naples that his cousin counseled him to deal with them harshly, even if it meant war. But Elzéar refused to inaugurate his administration with bloodshed, remaining convinced that gentleness and tact would ultimately undue their reproaches. And he was right. Calm and patience served him well. Another time, when he discovered among his deceased father's papers that a subordinate had attempted through libelous accusations to discredit the master's reputation and competence, Elzéar determined that forbearance compelled him to destroy the documentation. This he did, though Delphine, who had eventually joined him in Italy, was less inclined to do so and even felt that justice demanded appropriate retribution for what was a nonetheless persistent threat. Obviously, saintly judgments can differ. Elzéar showered the unruly opponent with affection, thereby winning the rival's esteem and support. Such was Elzéar's gentlemanly and congenial way. Clearly then Elzéar was an able and prudent manager.[23] His refined ethical standards were arresting; he managed with strict justice and never accepted bribes. Multitasking was second nature to him. Even while dedicated to his various philanthropic and charitable works, he admirably oversaw with a businessman's acumen those for whom

---

22. Bernard, *Époux vierges*, 22, 107.
23. Butler, *Lives*, 3:661–62; Bernard, *Époux vierges*, 126.

he was responsible politically.[24] Renown for such acumen was bound to endure.

SAINT FERDINAND III—AN EXEMPLARY COMMANDER WHO PRIZED SUBSIDIARITY

Thirteenth-century Spain was distinguished by the infamous if not glorious reign of this handsome, gifted, and formidable inheritor of royal dominion. By two beautiful queens, wives successively because of the first's unfortunate death, he enlivened his castles with thirteen children. Ferdinand's accession of León, a kingdom neighboring his Castilian domain, was no frictionless accomplishment. Contrary dispositions typically stand in the way of such politicking. In this case supporters of other claimants to the crown vigorously raised their voices. And the rest of the Iberian Peninsula was burdened by the turbulent discordance of several small kingdoms and relentless infighting among Christians. But Ferdinand was a royal leader of considerable political skill and notable prudence. As a force of unity he exhibited phenomenal efficacious dedication to the citizenry's wellbeing. He governed as his mother had counseled: "Kings must not live for themselves."[25]

Even as a youth in his father's court at León, he had studied the relevant legal and historical documents of his land. So he was familiar with nuanced application of law, especially for the sake of justice. And he did not take decisive action entirely on his own. Only what he considered the best among advisors and counselors could, he wisely averred, be included in his regal retinue, drawn from local governments, the military, the church, and the judiciary. For matters of eminent importance, such a cohort typically consisted of twelve hand-picked counselors. And to abet the finest results of whatever counsel he followed, he sought that an environment of justice should prevail overall, whether for foreign leaders or his own citizenry. His subjects should always sense that the royal entourage was treating them fairly; they should owe and pay their taxes but always ones that were fair and clearly needed. The policy was not only one tempered by justice but also by political expediency; for discontent among the citizenry could erode Ferdinand's royal authority.

---

24. Wikipedia, "Elzéar de Sabron," para. 3; Bernard, *Époux vierges*, 150; Giangrosso, "Hailigen Ellzearius," 141–42, 144.

25. Fitzhenry, *Saint Fernando III*, 164.

To these political and humanistic ends he initiated the formulation of a comprehensive set of laws. It would provide a unified legal system that would lessen the need for the king—as the ultimate arbiter of the land—to be totally familiar with the sundry jurisdictions of the kingdom. And Ferdinand spend many hours and days heeding the pleas of many for justice. His project therefore addressed matters of rightful ownership, fair commerce, defense, seafaring, litigation, and taxation. Parliamentary-style structures were encouraged; and internationally, diplomacy should outdo war whenever achievable. His efforts toward implementation of such a legal code would ultimately materialize under his son and royal successor.

Early in his kingly career Ferdinand had in fact resorted to military action in an effort to secure for his kingdom several towns illegally taken by a rival noble. Ferdinand succeeded, though with great effort. When the victory appeared to be only a temporary gain, he drew on diplomacy with fervor and wisdom in order to avoid further battle, and with that came a permanent nonviolent triumph.

Soon thereafter the young king began to fulfill his fervent dream of reclaiming all of Spain for Christianity. Initially he took, either by peaceful negotiation or fierce bloodshed, two or three Muslim-held towns in the large territory of Andalusia, south of his homeland. Such early victories, some quite hard won, continued. Muslims despaired; Christians rejoiced. In 1230 Ferdinand's father died, having stipulated in his will that his two daughters would succeed him as sovereigns of León. Despite influential local support for this arrangement, Ferdinand's mother, Berenguela, and the queen mother of the designated daughters peacefully negotiated a treaty. Ferdinand thereby became the king of a united Castile and León, a structure that he made permanent constitutionally.[26]

As an accomplished ruler he needed credibility and a leader's clout. These were essential to attaining a historically significant goal set by both religious and political interests. For he was keenly intent upon liberating Spain, by far the largest portion of the Iberian Peninsula, from what he believed was the destructive presence of the Muslims, typically called Moors at the time. Their religious and cultural Islamic grip on the kingdom appeared to him and many in his citizenry as the unjust repression of centuries-long Christian influence. Thus his wars against them, campaigns driven by religious rather than imperialistic sentiments,[27] seemed unending

---

26. Fitzhenry, *Saint Fernando III*, 164.
27. Butler, *Lives*, 2:426.

as they raged for some thirty years. The Catholic Church rewarded him with tithes and blessings originally designated for the eastern Crusades and with certain large territorial rights that allowed his rule in Spain to be extended considerably beyond Castile. Thus in unifying various regional governments under his single rule, Ferdinand not only enhanced the image of Spain but succeeded in acquiring more Muslim territory than anyone else in the Middle Ages.[28]

In battle Ferdinand was a fierce warrior, always seeking to exemplify fortitude and endurance in solidarity with his comrades in arms. As a young king, even before his marriage to his first wife Beatrice, he had pledged himself to valorous activity on behalf of his religion and his country. Thus he attained the noble rank of knighthood. It was a result of his aspirations to formidable and chivalrous service on behalf of his nation and church that the enormous swathes of Islamic-dominated territory in the southern Iberian Peninsula fell to his battling regiments. Nonetheless, Ferdinand's dispositions toward the vanquished were notably marked by generosity and magnanimity. Though many Muslims fled the conquered territories, Ferdinand never expelled any of them nor ever prohibited those who remained from peaceably professing and practicing their Islamic faith. Equally remarkable was his tolerant posture regarding Jews. It was a time in Spain when, by and large, Christians, Jews, and Muslims had heretofore been able to coexist in relative harmony. But gradually feelings of antipathy toward Muslims, increasingly regarded by Christians as oppressive, were on the rise.

In this context, where not only Christians opposed Muslims but when some Christians opposed one another (as did certain Muslims), Ferdinand strategically allied his army with that of the Muslim rival of the Muslim leader of Cordoba. He was particularly pleased in 1236 when his allied army took that renowned and imposing Muslim stronghold. Though temporarily afflicted with a serious illness after the victory, he would wage additional successful campaigns. The siege of Seville was formidably challenging. It was well defended and strategically crucial. Enlivening his tired troops by his example and encouragement, Ferdinand prevailed.[29] Eventu-

---

28. Beretz, "Ferdinand III of Castile."

29. Fernández, *King of Castile*, xi, 18–19, 30, 54–59, 61, 80–95, 105, 117, 154, 158, 172, 219, 253–56, 269–70.

ally he moved his royal home from Castile to Seville.[30] It was only the cities of Alicante and Granada that he never lived to see in Christian hands.

The centuries-long Christian retrieval of the Iberian Peninsula previously held by Muslims, the campaign known as the *Reconquista* or Reconquest, was thus substantially bolstered by Ferdinand. His part in this historic movement entailed not merely the suppression of Islamic influence but the monumental reinvigoration and development of Christian life and institutions as well. He facilitated the foundation of new dioceses, funded new monasteries, financed the building of hospitals, and financed the building of cathedrals in Toledo, Burgos, and León. The king was personally responsible for evoking among Santiagans the joy of hearing again the vibrant tones the beloved bells stolen from them by the Muslim Al-Mansur.[31] The symbolism of this restoration—the resounding proclamation of Christianity's return to full dignity—meant to the rest of Spain as much as any of Ferdinand's military victories.

The king amplified his devoted attention to his religion by subsidizing the embellishment of many churches with fine decor and furnishings. In addition he oversaw in the architectural transformation of renowned mosques into splendid Christian edifices, such as the Cathedral of St. Mary of the Assumption in Cordoba and the immense Cathedral of St. Mary of the See in Seville. Ferdinand also ordered that increased funds be provided for bishops so that the faithful in need could avail themselves of more charitable institutions, especially hospitals. The role of bishops thus had civil implications. So his support of them civilly complemented his satisfaction with their pastoral service, a practically inevitable eventuality in light of his concurrence in their appointment. In this regard Ferdinand, a loyal servant of his church, respectfully refused to comply with the papal request that he relinquish his traditional right to approve the ecclesiastical installation of bishops in his jurisdiction.[32] The king's motives were consistent with his altruism, not some regrettable authoritarianism.

After taking Cordoba, which was abandoned by its Muslim occupants, he did not retain its riches for himself but arranged to have them fairly distributed among his fellow warriors. The properties and lands were made available to those committed to working them, and many willing citizens of the peninsula's north came south to avail themselves of the opportunity.

---

30. Menocal, *Ornament of the World*, 199–200.
31. Arduino, "San Fernando III," para. 6.
32. Laurentie, *Saint Ferdinand*, 48, 50–52, 62, 76–77; Maccono, *Ferdinando III*, 67–68.

Making the Most of Things—Tenets and Tactics

Ferdinand acted similarly after taking Seville, though with his approval many Muslims remained in the city peaceably under his rule, while they were also allowed to serve dutifully in his army. Countless thousands of them however chose migration to northern Africa on ships Ferdinand provided or to other parts of southern Spain, again, with the king's assistance.[33] All the reconquered territory was able to profit in some way from population incentives prompted by royal generosity and political expediency.[34]

Complementing Ferdinand's humanitarian, religious, and civic interests was his commitment to science and the arts. Education in all the rest of Europe saw its rival emerge with Ferdinand's founding of the great University of Salamanca.[35] He also supported the great centers of learning at Valencia and Valladolid. He thus forged a united Spain into an eminent Christian nation. By his endearing qualities he came to be recognized as a model leader, one who proceeded according to sound principles and enduring wisdom.

SAINT MARGARET OF SCOTLAND—A QUEEN WITH ADMINISTRATIVE SENSE

Fleeing recently invaded England, the eleventh-century royal damsel unexpectedly found herself Scotland's queen. As the new wife of the nation's king she brought fresh color and contour to the palatial milieu. In the Scottish royal tradition, Margaret was an innovator in other ways. There is no historical record that any of her predecessors came close to exercising queenship in her unique manner. She was not merely the wife of the king but, as his partner, a leader in her own right, widely admired for her intelligence and eloquence.

Her servants and household fell under her distinctive care. Kindness and generosity were its shining features. She was like a kind mother whose guiding hand was firm but warm. Moved by such command, all the servants—women and men—held her in awe, were loyal in their duties, and demonstrable in their affection for her. Though a cheery person, she could display anger when offering correctives but always with a kind regard for the feelings of the offender. Though encouraging elegant menus, she was careful to dissuade certain knights at the royal table from gluttony. And

---

33. Maccono, *Ferdinando III*, 202-4.
34. Fitzhenry, *Saint Fernando III*, 100-101, 227, 325-26.
35. Heckmann, "St. Ferdinand III," 6.

when they too hastily left at meal's end, she diplomatically introduced a special cup of wine so that dining could be concluded with a due prayer of grace. They gladly concurred with her directive, and the Cup of Grace endured as a custom in the land for dozens of generations.

Her influence in the royal court led to notable governmental reforms. All laws of the land, she counseled, should be obeyed,[36] especially those affecting the administration of justice. With greater unity and streamlined organization, the offices of the throne could attend to the country's needs more fittingly and efficiently. In seeing to this she exhibited her reservations about oversize administration or government. In keeping with her character, such caution was rooted in her propensity to wield authority with a light hand, with respect for subjects' dignity. This procedure flowed not merely from principle but concurrently with practical sensitivity to her subjects, whom she knew firsthand, most likely by her accompanying the king on his extensive travels.

Queen Margaret greatly expanded trade in Scotland, encouraging her people to buy from a spectrum of venders, many of whom were from abroad.[37] Merchandising came to include jewelry, gold, and quite varied items of great worth and beauty. Many of these had never been seen in Scotland before but eventually came to affect Scottish culture. What we know today as Scottish plaid overtook the traditional simpler wools.[38] Her aesthetic eye effectively complemented her commercial expertise.

In other matters the talented young queen looked far beyond her household—namely, to all of Scotland—to promote the arts, education, and religious practice. Margaret fostered the appointment of competent teachers. She was foremost a great champion of the church. The practice of the Christian religion in Scotland had in many ways become rather lax. Her encouragement of reforms reflected her dedication to her religion and brought political advantages of more strongly aligning the church with the crown.[39] She not only instigated and encouraged meetings with church personnel to address pressing issues, she also attended them and participated in the proceedings. An ecclesiastical synod of bishops she initiated brought about reforms regarding the celebration of the liturgy, the practice of fasting during Lent, the taking of Communion during the Easter season, due

---

36. Turgot, *Dunfermline Vita*, 178.
37. Turgot, *Vita Margaretae*, 151–52.
38. Marshall, "Malcolm Canmore."
39. Keene, *Saint Margaret*, 50, 53, 60, 68–69.

observance of the Lord's Day, and marriage regulations regarding allowable degrees of relationship between the spouses.[40] To assist pastors—who she insisted should be respectable and competent—in providing edifying settings of worship, she organized the ladies of her court into a guild to provide suitably embroidered vestments and church furnishings.[41] Her promotion of the stunning and beautiful, as shone in dress, trappings, and decor, flowed well beyond the royal court and touched the populace as they relished the duties and joys of practicing their faith, particularly in the celebration of rituals. Thus her spiritual interests particularly illumined her splendorous and productive reign while enhancing the socioeconomic life of her people. Memory of her would not easily be blurred.

SAINT LOUIS IX—A MODEST KING WITH A HEART OF GOLD

Guided initially by his queen mother in earlier years, the mature Louis earned international prestige as an erudite and respected thirteenth-century French monarch. He ruled in splendor but with recognized reserve. One could hardly imagine a more amiable administrator. At home Louis was generous toward the servants of his and Queen Marguerite's household, showing them particular attention in their times of need. The whole assemblage enjoyed a kind of family spirit; whether in royal exercises of authority or submission to it, relationships within the royal palace were duly respectful of rank but rather casual. There prevailed in the royal court an air of propriety, so indecency of any kind was prohibited. Louis wore his kingship lightly, at times even humbly, yet always with an appropriate sense of his royal dignity.

Beyond the court he had heartfelt esteem for those formally or by vow living in religious communities, and he was ever responsive to such believers' expressions of need. With more than a dozen major gifts to the Franciscan and Dominican religious orders,[42] he financed the building of complexes for monks and nuns. At Royaumont, during his youthful years prior to marriage, he not only financed but physically assisted in building an abbey for the Cistercian monks, with whom he shared values and

---

40. Menzies, *St. Margaret*, 52, 55–56, 100–103, 153; Dunlop, *Queen Margaret of Scotland*, 61; Wilson, *St. Margaret*, 88.

41. Butler, *Lives*, 2:516–17.

42. Little, "Saint Louis' Involvement," 134.

companionship. During construction he personally helped carry stones and mortar while urging his attendants to do likewise. Here subordinates were gently but effectively motivated by a noble gentleman willing to get his hands dirty.

During his kingship he directed the building of Sainte-Chapelle on the royal estate in Paris to enshrine sacred relics dear to him and to Christianity generally, including the crown of thorns said to be worn by Jesus during his Passion, and revered fragments, such as those of the cross on which Jesus died. These Louis rescued through negotiators at Constantinople for a sum, some say, twice that of the costs for building the chapel. While it was the wealth of Louis's kingdom that made this possible, it was the king's faith that made it a reality. For he was convinced that such an investment, by nurturing faith, truly benefitted France. The chapel was a masterpiece; its renowned magnificence displayed Louis's enthusiasm for expression in the Gothic style. Such patronage had a ripple effect on art and architecture throughout the continent, and throughout the coming ages.

Attentive to the social need for justice, King Louis exhorted his emissaries to gather complaints of the populace throughout France so that injustices could be remedied.[43] He himself regularly presided over juridical proceedings conducted for the good of his people. Here the presumption of innocence until proven guilty prevailed. He was renowned for his personal judgments under an oak tree of the nearby Vincennes woods or in the royal garden of his Parisian palace. In disputes between someone rich and someone poor, he favored paying particular attention to the poor person, estimating that the rich person already enjoyed considerable hearing. Once, imposing for a terribly heinous crime a sizable fine leaving a rich man nearly bankrupt, Louis ordered the sum to be designated for charity. He was demonstrably and indefatigably devoted to his church, but his aversion to injustice prompted him to pursue even cases brought against bishops.

Louis's sense of justice was evident in his social policy. Much of the king's revenue came as proceeds from the royal forests and from fair and moderate taxation. It has been argued that in Saint Louis's times the established feudal economy was gradually giving way to a more "capitalistic" one where competition and expanding markets played large roles.[44] The growth of cities was marked by the flourishing of new labor skills and means of

---

43. Vauchez, *Laity*, 23.
44. See Sivery, *Economie du royaume*; Le Goff, *Saint Louis*, 546, 561.

production. The development of local governments or councils paralleled the emergence of a new middle class. Not directly concerned with debates about labor and commerce, the king implicitly accepted what we would call today a free market. Nonetheless his caution against exploitation, like excessive interest on loans, was quite lively, as was his dedication to justice in all commercial interactions.

Louis admonished his son Philip to support the realm's noble traditions while vanquishing adherence to ignoble ones. The prince, he said, should not—later, as sovereign—be seeking gain for himself, nor afflicting taxation on the citizenry on his own behalf, except in extreme necessity. Moderation and prudence in governance were imperative. The one at the royal helm, Louis advised, should enjoy the frequent counsel of those, clerical or lay, whose loyalty is civic minded and not self-serving. Those of lesser ilk should be avoided. For the company and guidance of admirable friends and associates, noted Louis, was essential to the king's living according to his values, cherishing righteousness, and abhorring iniquity in all their forms.

By such leadership the king, noted Louis, should foster such dispositions in all his subjects, whether of his household or of his realm. This would be especially important in urban and other municipal areas. Where digression from noble traditions and establishments is evident, adjustments should be made in ways that heighten the citizens' heartfelt commendation of their king. Thus the enormous political and economic influence of the great urban centers will create a climate wherein the citizenry and immigrants—and especially the king's local representatives—will be reluctant to offer him resistance in any way. So the king should regularly inquire of domestic supervisors and local authorities whether they have succumbed in any way to distortions, duplicity, or undue aspirations.[45] Admirable leadership requires an admirable administrative team.

Though from his teen years a skilled military leader, in territorial disputes he preferred negotiation to conquest. When required to battle and proving victorious, he demonstrated mercy and leniency toward the enemy. He viewed conquest as a blessing of peace for his people, a wondrous divine grace,[46] since during his reign the territory of France expanded considerably.

---

45. de Joinville, *Life of St. Louis*, 214–16.
46. Butler, *Lives*, 3:394–98.

Good and Wealthy

In the area of education Louis encouraged the founding of the Sorbonne, providing it with a sizable endowment. This new university in Paris was originally intended for the poor, and would soon house a renowned theological faculty claiming such professorial greats as the saintly Bonaventure, Albert the Great, and Thomas Aquinas. Louis particularly valued the works of Aquinas and in many ways embodied Aquinas's political theology.[47]

In 1254 Louis issued the "Great Ordinance," a measure aiming at enhanced economic justice—especially for the poor—and at more effectively safeguarding morality and Christian teachings. The decree was to be enforced fairly by honorable and reputable officers throughout the kingdom.[48] They were to see that justice prevailed in all cases, irrespective of any litigant's status or influence; any submission to bribery was to be completely avoided. They were to conduct themselves as gentlemen at all times, even desisting from blasphemy and gambling. Since justice throughout France was always to prevail by royal principles, private wars and judicial duels (settling disputes by personal combat when there were no witnesses to the incident in question) were forbidden.[49] Women and their rights were to be specially protected. Prostitution was severely restricted to safeguard public propriety.

In the midst of such prevailing principles of justice and administration, Louis's aversion to aspects of Judaism has not gone unnoticed or unmentioned. It stands out in the royal histories as one of the king's noticeable traits. To the extent that the king's disposition can be called anti-Semitic, it is consonant, sadly, with Christians' practice of the day but by later Christian standards deemed particularly reprehensible. Louis opposed heresies within his own religion and opposed Jewish teachings he saw as also adverse to his own religion. Like fellow believers of his and preceding centuries, Louis lamented the Jewish rejection of Jesus as the Messiah. Thus he encouraged burnings of the Talmud and ordered deportations of Jews deemed especially threatening. Yet he respected Judaism as a true religion, one worshiping the same God as Christianity and sharing with it the Old Testament.[50] Though he legislated against the usury commonly practiced by Jews and required them to wear a marking of their religion, he largely

---

47. Cantor, *Middle Ages*, 450.
48. Richard, *St. Louis*, 80, 156–63.
49. Folz, *Saints roi*, 108, 169.
50. See Wikipedia, "Louis IX," sec. "Mesures prises contre les Juifs."

regarded them as a minority worthy of protection from injustice or any harm and facilitated restitution for pillaging of their synagogues, while heartily seeking their conversion to Christianity. These approaches—ambiguous as they were—along with Louis's overwhelming evidence of an otherwise virtuous and exemplary Christian life, were enough to elicit overwhelmingly favorable dispositions from his contemporaries and earn for him the title of *saint* from those who survived him.[51] He was treasured for his lifetime of saintly achievements—not judged solely by a notable flaw. To a sovereign who showed mercy, mercy was granted. The king had a good heart. And the streams of charity that flowed from it strikingly outshone concurrent ripples of weakness and vulnerability. The manifold contours of his sanctity emerged in bold relief, as we will see.

VENERABLE PIERRE TOUSSAINT—MASTER OF HIS TRADE, ADMIRED CITIZEN

He was a successful black St. Domingan immigrant to New York City while the United States was enjoying the first decades of its independence. Racial prejudice was practically nonexistent in certain sectors there, especially in the white society of French heritage. Moreover, in the busy eighteenth-century American port city, many even among the white population of other heritages, were unaffected by his blackness and afforded him kindness, respect, and admiration. It seems that common interests among associates weighed more than color. Pierre brought courtesy, kindness, and cheer to his trade. The French he had learned as a boy graced his speech with fluid elegance. The English that he mastered in New York bore delicate hues of a French accent. By his pleasantly reserved and diplomatic presence he gained from his customers a confidence in which they delighted. Several were pleased to regard him as a dear friend. Many of them, including some of the black servants of his white clientele, welcomed his counsel, recommendations, and good humor. Such relationships complemented his distinguished art of hairdressing and his savvy as a businessman.

Industrious Pierre was notoriously successful in a profession where there was abundant competition. Keenly attentive to the ever-changing fashion, he masterfully provided every coiffure that was the rage of the day. But he was also creative. His signature design was a magnificent coiffure donned with a vibrant flower. Working seventy to eighty hours a week, he

---

51. Le Goff, *Saint Louis*, 79, 100, 159, 533–46, 561, 570–71, 650–67.

adorned the heads of young ladies for first communions, and readied the hair of maturer belles for weddings, christenings, balls, and funerals. One client engaged him not only to cut a boy's hair but also to instruct him in social etiquette. Another customer even enjoined him to give her children dancing lessons.

From contact with successful families he learned of profits from investments. Astute as he was, he channeled some of his funds into real estate, banking, and insurance. When at times, because of his color, such dealing was inadmissible, someone else kindly posed in his stead as the investor. Importing and selling selected commodities also enlarged Pierre's interests. These and similar ventures steadily contributed to his ever-increasing income. At the peak of his career he lost almost everything when a devastating New York fire brought claims depleting the funds of insurance companies in which he had multiple investments. But the loss was only temporary, not depriving him, or his wife Juliette, of their industriousness, determination, and faith. The Toussaint couple's typical activities continued, including loans and gifts to those in need. Juliette and Pierre's productive, joyous lives were scarcely impacted by the financial loss. Before and, in time, after the fire many counted them among the wealthiest New Yorkers. It was no surprise therefore that Pierre left his heirs a substantial fortune.[52]

Pierre was a welcome conversationalist and counselor, as well as an avid correspondent. A large collection of letters reveal his refined entrepreneurial skills and his warmhearted interest in others. He kept his own records meticulously and resolved that he would never be in debt, though he occasionally deferred for a limited time full payment on a bill and thus incurred some interest. Busy sometimes sixteen hours a day, he practiced his trade in his shop but mostly in his customers' homes. Though he was not allowed on the public carriages because of his color, he happily moved with his tools from house to house and drew pleasant gazes by his jaunty gate and happy disposition.

But always, especially at night, he had to be cautious. As a black man, he could be accosted or even kidnapped and sold into slavery. The same horrid possibility loomed for his wife and their niece. Fortunately his clients and friends, most of whom were white, did not succumb to bigotry. Many of them were of French heritage, and French New Yorker's were quite welcoming of racial diversity. Never restrained by fear, Pierre maintained

---

52. Jones, *Pierre Toussaint*, 153–54, 172, 183, 196–99, 208, 272, 274–75, 277, 281–84, 288, 295, 300.

Making the Most of Things—Tenets and Tactics

the habit of walking even in later times when some carriages were reserved for the "colored," though in his last few years he developed an arthritic knee that made him limp. The decades of regular exercise may have contributed to his impressive longevity and apparent resistance to illness.[53] He lived during the consecutive terms of fourteen presidents of the United States.

At five-foot-nine he was quite tall for his times. Modest earrings complemented his always fashionable dress, and on the job his speckless apron signaled a meticulous professional. Though racism was common enough in certain quarters of New York, he never felt degraded for being black or a nominal slave. He in fact, with pronounced serenity, regarded himself as the equal of anyone else. Racial equality, he felt, prevailed by providential design.

Graciousness and generosity were hallmarks of the Toussaint home. When Pierre's sister died, he and Juliette adopted her orphaned infant daughter. Grateful for the training and education he had received in his youth, Pierre helped his niece in self-appreciation, domestic responsibility, and development of her religious faith. He taught her how to read and write in both English and French, empowering her to become through her letters something of a crack reporter on New York events, before tuberculosis claimed her young teen life.[54] Having grieved terribly over the loss of this adopted child so dear to him, he turned with new energy to helping others out of impoverishment or the threat of it. Sometimes it was merely a matter of temporary financial assistance attained through fundraising fairs or raffles that he organized on behalf of those in dire financial need, such as orphans or widows. He and Juliette fostered several children whom they prepared for adult life by teaching them financial independence. A celebrated master of connecting people with work, he once helped a French woman out of financial distress by facilitating her ability to teach conversational French to the children of some New York scholars. In all such deeds of charity, his wife Juliette remained a companion and partner.[55] Pierre regarded her fully as his equal, as the matriarchal strand of his African heritage would have inclined him.[56] She was a notable counterpart of a man whose sanctity would become increasingly evident.

---

53. Tarry, *Pierre Toussaint*, 203, 275, 286, 288, 333, 366; Jones, *Pierre Toussaint*, 12.

54. Hanley, "Pierre Toussaint," paras. 53, 75, 77.

55. Lee, *Memoir of Pierre Toussaint*, 17, 35, 56–57, 59, 68–70, 74–77, 82, 110.

56. Jones, *Pierre Toussaint*, 72, 117–18, 143–45, 174, 193, 201–3, 234–35, 237, 240, 244, 289, 317.

BLESSED FRÉDÉRIC OZANAM—PRACTICAL ORGANIZER AND INSPIRING THEORIST

Family background, personal proclivities, extensive travel, and strenuous study coalesced in the productive life of Professor Ozanam. With amiable reservation he relished the finer things of life. And with charming modesty this French intellectual enjoyed academic renown and the admiration of an international audience of readers. His accomplishments rode on the wave of his astounding insights and well-honed skills.

The discussion group that Frédéric founded in the 1830s during his study of law at the University of Paris soon moved from theory to practice. The notion of service as inherent to Christianity prompted roughly seven of the members to found the Conference of Charity, which brought needed goods and encouragement to the area's poor. The model for the group was St. Vincent de Paul, who had done much in France some two centuries earlier to help those in need. In a little more than a year the conference membership, now named the Society of St. Vincent de Paul, grew to one hundred. While several members were involved in the society's founding, Frédéric came to be celebrated as the principle founder since he most clearly embodied the group's ideals and most inspired the membership to carry out its mission. He also undoubtedly influenced the formulation of the rule by which the society is governed to this day. His stipulations included the members' regularly circulating among themselves letters that facilitated transparency, accountability, and mutual encouragement. Such letters manifestly helped preserve the essence of the group's original spirit.

The friendship among the members was notable if not palpable. Frédéric considered this bond essential to the society's work, and his principle would be valued well into the group's future. For the friendship the members enjoyed among themselves provided a template for the bond they would hopefully establish with those they served. It soon became evident however that the demands of charity itself invited the conference to a partial sacrifice of members' common friendship; the bonds between them needed to include acquaintanceship, bonding the members realistically in their common commitment to charity. Thus the expanding society became more bureaucratic while its governance became more democratic. The group was initially guided by a nun, Sister Rosalie Rendu, renowned throughout Paris for her beneficence and herself named blessed in 2003. She was experienced in organized charitable work, and the membership quickly grew to another hundred visiting and helping the poor. During

Making the Most of Things—Tenets and Tactics

those early years slightly more than 90 percent of the members were from the middle and upper classes.

Frédéric began his career of charitable service by delivering his personal stock of firewood to a poor widow.[57] The practice of assisting the poor in their homes—an approach encouraged by St. Vincent de Paul de Paul—was already established among French middle class or bourgeois women as a way of building rapport between socioeconomic classes. Frédéric's mother had been one of such charitable ladies.[58] Now the in-home visit was a hallmark of the services rendered by Frédéric and his confreres. Thus the men of the society learned from charitable women, especially Sister Rosalie, the value of a personal and even amicable touch. Frédéric became persuaded that rendering to the poor not only material assistance but also comfort, emotional support, and warm friendship was requisite to the work of the society.[59] Its manner of establishing personal relationships with the poor was in his view charity in its best sense and thus distinguishable from public or governmental support such as welfare assistance. Frédéric in fact favored both sectarian and public forms of social concern but fostered in the society the conviction that faith-inspired charity was an absolutely essential supplement to purely humanitarian welfare assistance. To safeguard propriety the men soon adopted the principle of visiting women's homes in pairs. A year after its formal organization, as the members graduated and followed their professions, there were branches of the group in other French cities and in Rome.

The talent, interests, publications and skills that impelled Frédéric toward a professorate in Paris served him well there. His lectures were inspiring and provocative, evoking excitement and cheers. Hungering for more of his wisdom, students would engulf him as he strolled on his way home across the Luxembourg Gardens. The students' enthusiastic progress meant more to him than their adulation. Except on his lecture days, he devoted two hours of his school schedule to advising students who eagerly waited outside his office for their turns to confer with him. Convinced that friendliness to the poor was essential to the work of his society, he brought the same amiability to his commitments as a teacher. What the students emulated was his agility at attending to their concerns while intertwining sound academic perspectives with attention to effective social objectives.

---

57. Wikipedia, "Frédéric Ozanam," para. 5.
58. de Dinechin, *Frédéric Ozanam*, 54, 61.
59. Bernardelli, *Storia*, 129.

This highly challenging and time-consuming combination in all of Frédéric's work was largely facilitated by the loving support of his wife Amalie.[60] Significant sectors of the society's organization and development were in her hands. And she frequently accompanied him on visits to the poor.[61]

As an advocate of political and labor reform in 1848, he laid the groundwork for a policy of a sufficient wage justly proportionate to an employer's profit, provoked consideration of unemployment and accident insurance, and proposed a program of guaranteed pensions. Such considerations were later woven into the highly influential papal encyclical on social rights and responsibilities, Leo XII's *Rerum novarum*. Frédéric argued that service to an exploitative employer was a form of enslavement.[62] In his view a suitable wage would, say, allow parents of two children to adequately shelter, clothe, and feed the family while providing support and health care for the couple's own retired parents.[63] This would surely challenge many an employer. Yet Frédéric was opposed to socialism, which he regarded as a tired old materialist ideology that unduly raised hopes because its ideas were inadequately justified.[64] He averred that in socialism, with its denial of competition and thus liberty, government mirrors the oppression of a cruel plantation.[65] Though never engaged as a politician, he continued to voice his proposals journalistically, and to encourage the widespread practice of charity through the Society of St. Vincent de Paul, which by 1848 had grown to nearly four hundred local groupings.[66]

Frédéric faced days when, not able to pen a word, he longed for freedom from what he regarded as the challenges of writing. Yet his concern for social ills became eminently expressed in the political, philosophical, and theological terms that nonetheless embellish his manifold theoretical publications. Correspondingly his rapport with creative genius sensitive to imagery in life's color and contours allowed his writing craft to blossom in his compelling literary studies. While remarkably tolerant of a broad range of perspectives, he held steadfastly to his own faith, indeed loving it with

---

60. Butler and Burns, *Lives*, 420–22.
61. Harrison, *Romantic Catholics*, 201–5, 216–17.
62. Honner, *Love and Politics*, 53–61, 74.
63. Mousin, "Frédéric Ozanam," 69–70.
64. Sickinger, *Antoine Frédéric Ozanam*, 73, 83, 139, 170, 181–83, 189, 192, 212–13, 224, 243–45.
65. Bernardelli, *Storia*, 104.
66. Slattery, *Blessed Frederic Ozanan*, 5–6, 9–10.

a passion. Though astutely conversant in it, whenever his writing touched on matters of religion, he had his work checked for orthodoxy by a reliable theologian.[67] Animated by hands-on assistance to the poor, his publications and leadership in the Society of St. Vincent de Paul energized its groups, which, in turn, became magnets for droves, especially among younger populations. By 1852 the society mushroomed into two thousand conferences on five continents.[68] All such achievements would become in him the stuff of extraordinary virtue, the content of blessedness, the emblems of sanctity.

BLESSED VICTOIRE RASOAMANARIVO— A KINDLY EXECUTIVE

The island now known as Madagascar can look with pride to one of its wealthiest and celebrated personalities. She enjoyed luxury modestly, witnessed to exemplary virtue in a stressful marriage, was admired for her philanthropy, and during a period of oppression earned adulation for heroic efforts to preserve the expression of Christianity to which she had committed herself. Her extraordinary achievements however were unadorned by flamboyance or pretense.

Victoire's domestic demeanor included benevolence toward her slaves. In the culture of Madagascar during the nineteenth century, there was a clear class distinction between slaves and free persons. Yet it was not unusual for a slave to be treated almost like family and enjoy privileged positions, such as, in Victoire's home, being given oversight of the household and possession of its keys. Even as a teen in school Victoire had displayed deference and kind consideration of slaves. Now, in her own household, her deference to them continued, though she would at times appropriately reprimand them for unneighborly conduct. By dressing suitably for her status but unpretentiously, she refrained from highlighting class discrimination. She made sure that the slaves had appropriate food, clothing, and wages. The household slaves were mostly children, and Victoire saw to their care and education like a loving mother, though she and her husband never had children of their own.

Class division meant nothing to her. If a slave was ill or tired to near incapacity, Victoire would assume his or her chores, whether they involved cleaning or gardening. And she personally provided the sick slave with care.

67. Baunard, *His Correspondence*, 24, 72, 297–98, 306.
68. Rybolt, "Virtuous Personality," 39, 41–42.

She never required her slaves to address her formally since the household under her sister-like leadership functioned more familiarly than hierarchically. The laughter, song, and dance that filled the house included the company of the slaves. Often when her husband was away, she dined with them and even played games such as dominoes. When the slaves dined with her, she served them herself, and they were allowed to speak freely.[69] They were so endeared to her that two whom she freed refused to leave her. One of her slaves served her devotedly, even maternally, for a decade. When she died Victoire's tears were like those of a grieving daughter.[70]

Her benignity extended beyond her household. One of the leaders who served the Madagascar Catholic community in the absence of priests and nuns was a vowed religious brother. He tended to manage his particular sector rather autocratically. In face of the group's dissension Victoire intervened and restored harmony but only after publicly confronting the brother. By her diplomatic but firm manner, the work of the group was able to be reinvigorated. With her greater sense of the needs served by the group, she personally reached out to far-flung areas of its influence. Keenly aware of ever-multiplying exigencies, she succeeded in eliciting greater financial support for the entire operation.[71] Her boundless benevolence and creative leadership would hardly escape those who would come to revere her enduringly.

SAINTS LOUIS AND MARIE-AZÉLIE MARTIN— PRODUCTIVE AND ADMIRED PARTNERS

Louis and Zélie were successful entrepreneurs in quite different businesses, though artistry was the common denominator. She, the young executive in a lacemaking industry, and he, the gallant proprietor of a widely admired watch and jewelry enterprise, found their way to one another as their paths crossed on a decorous city bridge. The match led to marriage in 1858 and eventually to wedding business interests. He followed her lead in expanding the market of their keenly sought wares. And when she passed away, he furthered her devoted style of parenting.

---

69. Simon-Perret, *Victoire Rasoamanarivo*, 54–56.
70. Fourcadier, *Vie héroïque*, 9–10, 30, 47–48, 52–54.
71. Marie, "August 8, 2008," para. 15.

Making the Most of Things—Tenets and Tactics

Louis fully partnered with Zélie after he sold his original business.[72] They both loved their work and meticulously pursued it with great professionalism. Because of their indefatigable and competitive spirits, their product was widely prized. With a creative eye for fine material, Louis brought to the lace industry the same propensity for artistry that served him well in watchmaking. The company's fabric—made of scrupulously worked first-rate threads—never wanted for customers. Louis understood the market well enough to match maximization of sales to the company's potential. Zélie managed production adroitly, though at times she found it emotionally and physically tiring.[73] Alert for possibly sound investments, she sought counsel before pursing them. She once observed that Louis was someone who never aspired to riches. That was true. As a careful businessman he sought profit but avoided the risk of loss through speculative investment and was cautious about overextending sales.[74]

Louis also fully partnered with Zélie in parenting. She nurtured and taught the children with unflagging energy. Her tenderness toward them was warm and deep. Education, dress, and manners were high on her list of concerns for her children, all girls. Louis was generous in spending play time with them, engrossing them with the clatter of glistening marbles, amusing them with artful mimicry, or inspiring them as he gave voice to his collection of songs. As a watchmaker in his earlier years, Louis learned to appreciate jewelry and fine metals. And he lovingly translated these interests into nicknames for his daughters, who became his "diamond" and "pearl," or "angel" and "queen," and who themselves knew how to enjoy life's treasures.[75]

The Martins fashioned an especially happy home. All the children attested to that.[76] Warmth and esteem were not just limited to their children. The whole Martin family, the younger members guided by the parents, kindly regarded and treated employees and servants as family. Louis always carefully selected them for their edifying dispositions as well as their skills. In the view of Zélie, their generous wages should be rightfully complemented by the family's esteem. With heartfelt consideration she was careful to never overwork any employees, being mindful to work as hard as they did

---

72. Renda, introduction to *Deeper Love*, xxiv.
73. Office of the Postulator General of the Discalced Carmelites, "Profile," para. 19.
74. Louis Martin and Zélie Martin, *Deeper Love*, 87, 136, 140, 145.
75. Wikipedia, "Louis Martin and Marie-Azélie Guérin," para. 7.
76. Di Nicola and Danese, *Amore scritto in cielo*, 107–8, 110, 127.

Good and Wealthy

and even to nurture them when they were ill. At her death, one of the Martins' maids wept and attested to her kindness and sense of justice. Though bereft of Zélie, Louis and his daughters maintained her disposition toward servants even in the later household in Lisieux.[77] It was no surprise then that the servants there too spoke most highly of him.[78] The Martins were a couple who evoked not only praise but also heartfelt devotion. Such dispositions served what would eventually become the pair's universal renown.

SAINT GIANNA BERETTA MOLLA—INTENT ON SERVICE

Sadness and loss were not foreign to Gianna. Both of her parents passed away when she was twenty, and her oldest sister, so dear to her, died at the age of twenty-six.[79] Yet Gianna was by and large a happy and vivacious woman, having lived during the mostly early decades of twentieth-century Italy. She was a talented and ambitious student, from her younger years and all through her university semesters. In young adulthood her devotion to humanitarian service, especially by service to the poor as a member of the Society of St. Vincent de Paul,[80] broadened into assistance for teens and the elderly. In helping to train young people for volunteer service she offered support and counsel while intently heeding their numerous queries. She strove always when appropriate to communicate—literally—with a smile, with a sign of spiritual joy, with an expression that could uplift and invigorate.[81] This was a disposition that she retained from childhood.

Having become a physician and surgeon, she founded a clinic in Mesero. Though it was still somewhat unusual for a woman to be practicing medicine, she attracted many patients. She approached them with warm compassion, noting to her peers that faith and humane concern should outdo income as motivators for medically serving others.[82] Her time at the office each day ended only after all had been suitably treated. She even extended her professional hours into the night, visiting the sick in their homes when they needed her.[83] After her marriage to Pietro, he always went

---

77. Piat, *Story of a Family*, 168–73, 274.
78. Louis Wust and Marjorie Wust, *Louis Martin*, 68, 194.
79. Burke, "Saint Gianna Beretta Molla."
80. Epple, "Women of Faith," 347.
81. Da Riese Pio X, *Love of Life*, 105–6.
82. Guerriero, introduction to *Journey of Our Love*, 8–9.
83. Brown, *No Greater Love*, 8, 16.

Making the Most of Things—Tenets and Tactics

with her—she with her iconic smile[84]—on such nighttime calls. Beside her commitments to her regular patients, she donated her time to treating children as she pursued a medical specialization in pediatrics.

Gianna regarded her attention to patients as a healing touch that, by its spiritual motivation, served both their bodies and their souls. When she observed that patients' immoral or unhealthy behavior was contributing to their illnesses, she did not blush to counsel gainful change. She supported poorer patients with food and medicine. Firmly pro-life, she kindly attempted to dissuade individuals inclined to abortion but tenderly companioned without judgment those who had availed themselves of it, assuring them of divine mercy.[85]

Her mission as a medical professional always harmonized with dedication as a wife, mother, and community volunteer.[86] The conversations she enjoyed with Pietro, typically at a dinner she had prepared after a day at work, reflected appreciation of the perspectives that each brought to the other's accounts of the day, hers as a doctor and his as an engineer.[87] Gianna was an excellent cook, as numerous guests in the Molla home attested.[88] With the birth of the couple's third child, the increasing stress that she felt from juggling household management, child-rearing, and medical work became increasingly evident, much to Pietro's chagrin. Though hesitantly, she promised him that after the next child she would devote herself to full-time mothering.[89] What lay ahead would add to her sanctity but also to humanity's lament.

BLESSEDS LUIGI AND MARIA BELTRAME QUATTROCCHI—EMINENTLY REFINED AND EMINENTLY ENGAGED

As youngsters still nested with their families, Luigi and Maria followed their parents to Rome. Yet their paths converged and led to marriage, family, publishing, and public service—a trajectory that spanned the first half of the twentieth century. Having moved with his adoptive parents to the Italian capital at the age of eleven, Luigi's university studies equipped him

---

84. Allegri, *Due madri*, 49.
85. Pastoral Centre, "Life of St. Gianna Beretta Molla," para. 12.
86. Vatican News, "Gianna Beretta Molla (1922-1962)," para. 13.
87. Wallace and Jablonski, *Saint Gianna*, 31–32, 48–49.
88. Molla and Guerriero, *Saint Gianna Molla*, 68.
89. Pelucchi, *Saint Gianna*, 58–60, 76, 91.

to launch a legal career. Complementing his interest in law were his refined taste for classical Latin and Greek literature as well as the literary masterpieces of France, England, and his Italian homeland. Notable too was his enthusiasm for music and theater. He wore his refined legal expertise, polished eloquence, and lofty ethical standards noticeably but lightly, in a way that made him widely welcome, not only as a colleague but also as a friend. Thus his achievements were due not only to his professional competencies but also to the relationships he enjoyed, many of which were with prominent political and religious personalities.

His resume is extraordinarily impressive and seemingly endless. But his success in several significant areas of national political responsibility was not always without challenges. When one particularly high office was denied him because of nefarious intrigues of an anti-religious opponent, he felt the hurt deeply but did not openly dispute the result. His faith and professionalism allowed him to simply remain steadfast in face of such marginalization and thus render it only temporarily effectual.

While at business school in Rome, Maria mastered accounting and expanded her language skills to include English and French. Her love of literature led her as well to explore and enjoy its vast treasures in these languages. Dante, Shakespeare, Corneille, along with their likes, enriched and refined her gifted and curious mind. She was also talented musically, able to compellingly entertain at the piano. Elegant drawings and miniatures displayed her artistic talent. Marriage to Luigi, and eventually the lovely family that they produced, allowed her to develop her wifely and motherly skills. She was a model housekeeper, meticulously attentive to detail. Financial matters were in her hands, though she and Luigi concurred on major choices.

Early in their marriage they lived with Maria's elders. The tenderness that her parents displayed, along with the religious values to which the older couple witnessed, contributed immeasurably to the sensitivity and formation of their grandchildren. Virtue abounded. Hospitality was a hallmark of the home, where attention to guests—who often stayed overnight—was marked by kindness, edifying conversation, and thoughtfully prepared meals. Maria and Luigi extended such welcoming not only to countless Catholic acquaintances and dignitaries, but to Protestants, Jews, Masons, and Marxists, all of whom steadily visited and enjoyed courteous interaction in the energizing setting.

Making the Most of Things—Tenets and Tactics

The couple's days and years essentially passed with marked tranquility. There were however stressful periods. In response to needs of her community and country, Maria provided extensive, energetic service and leadership. Aside from such physical and mental toil, Maria never worked outside the home, where she produced her extensive writings. She considered her duties as wife and mother as part of a religious vocation, one that she embraced throughout married life and that she accepted with regard to even her grown children by offering them her continued welcome counsel. Yet she was in no way constrained to allow such sense of service to deplete her of the talents with which she was likewise endowed, ones that directed her attention outside family matters and into societal ones. In the midst of pressing responsibilities as a wife, mother, and daughter, she adroitly drew on her professional skills to write numerous well-received articles, books, and translations. Such productivity by a middle-class stay-at-home mom of her status was in those times hardly typical.[90]

Her first book, on motherly parenting, stressed the unique importance of the mother's role in the moral and religious education of the children, including sex education. She sees these areas as particularly important in an age of accented individualism. So all children, both girls and boys, should see in their mother an eminent authority equal with their father, who indeed should share in her work with like dedication. Subsequent publications, dealing with various expressions of religiousness, gave particular attention to children's spiritual formation and to awakening in them spiritual sensitivity. In a work specially directed to youth, she makes eminently clear that they must above all intently harken to the divine voice within and effectively act upon it. Drawing on experience in her own home and with children involved in her communal work, Maria's sublime and practical recommendations were widely well received. In her final publications, likewise eliciting widespread appreciation, Marie lucidly treats various stages and aspects of adult spirituality. Throughout her life and writings she reflects the perspectives of classical spiritual writers such as Francis of Assisi, Catherine of Siena, Therese of Lisieux, and Ignatius of Loyola.

Maria and Luigi also complemented their established professional and academic interests with graduate studies in religion at a famed Roman university. After the challenging and life-threatening fourth pregnancy, they began to abstain from sex. It was a religious choice, common at the time,[91]

---

90. Abbate, *Gesù é il mio unico*, 150, 155.
91. Catapano and Angrisani, *Mistica coniugale*, 16, 129.

though a challenging pursuit; it was one however that scarcely diminished their love[92] but instead brought them into fresh domains of intimacy and sensitivity.

By word and example they fostered a vibrant spirit of patriotism in the entire family.[93] When their four children were old enough to be suitably cared for in part by a household staff, the couple for a time worked in support of Italian Fascism. They were apparently influenced by their fervid patriotism, a sense of civic duty, and their allegiance to the Vatican, which, in the prevailing European turmoil, for a time chose alignment with Fascism as the least of several possible social evils, including Communism. The couple's political activity favoring Mussolini was not long-lived however. As the Fascist regime initiated policies and laws promoting racial discrimination and anti-Semitism, their disenchantment led to their total disapproval.[94] When offered the highest office he had ever attained, that of Italy's advocate general, Luigi declined, refusing to cooperate with the Fascist regime.[95]

After Italian support of Hitler reversed, he and Maria risked their lives by participating in a resistance movement, rescuing many from the horrors of Nazi invasion forces.[96] The Beltrame Quattrocchi home became a haven where many fleeing religious or political persecution—Jews, soldiers, and officials—could find refuge or generous assistance, while the enemy troops constantly hovered dangerously nearby.[97] Many of those fleeing certain capture or death at enemy hands were led away to safer areas. The harboring pair and their adult children resourcefully provided counterfeit documents or even disguises such as their children's religious garb.[98] Maria and Luigi, not a couple whose life engagement is easily abbreviated, adroitly set their sights on the near and the far, even beyond the boundaries of this world.

---

92. O'Neel, *Thirty-Nine New Saints*, 132, 134.
93. Beltrame Quattrocchi, *Lui, lei, noi, loro*, 20, 45–50, 71, 87, 91–92, 94.
94. Vanzan, "Maria e Luigi Beltrame Quattrocchi," 254.
95. Dell'Orto, *Sant'insieme*, 2.2.2; 2.2.4.
96. Savior.org, "Blessed Luigi Beltrame Quattrocchi," paras. 10, 14.
97. Beltrame Quattrocchi, *Ordito e la trama*, 31; Papàsogli, *Quesi borghesi*, 14–15, 21, 52–53, 115–16, 183, 190–91, 233–34, 257, 268–69, 339–51.
98. Pasquale, *Luigi e Maria*, 27.

CHAPTER 4

Living Fully—Godly Energy

THE VARIED LIVES AND impressive fortunes of the saintly persons presented here exhibit alluring and instructive features. These prominent women and men wore their wealth lightly, enjoyed it modestly, sometimes merely dutifully, without its becoming noxiously decorous. It never depraved them with offensive snobbery, pernicious power, or smug elitist hauteur. Amid abundance they shone like jewels in precious settings. Indeed riches brought enormous influence, a sway that these saintly personalities wielded with a respected leader's dignity and with refined consideration of others' rights and needs. Peers, employees, subjects, and the less fortunate variously profited from them, whose notable wealth was paired with the leaven of virtue. To this leaven we now specifically turn. It is multifaceted but suffused throughout with a specific nature, a spiritual substance that allows those so endowed to be wealthy *and* good. Their stories now take a uniquely inspiring turn, showing us why they could accomplish the supposedly unthinkable—namely, attaining by heavenly grace celestial heights of manner more easily than a laden camel passing through the eye of a needle.

SAINT GUNTRAM—A SCHMOOZING, KINDLY PUBLIC SERVANT

This sixth-century Burgundian king, a potentate of the old Frankish kingdom, grew up in the plush surroundings of nobility. His early life, scandalous and untamed, gave way to a practiced equanimity. He was thus able in his maturity to resist, whether in administration or war, corrupting

Good and Wealthy

influences of wealth and power. His admirers, both contemporaneously and in later ages, saw in him the features of a saint.

Guntram eventually repented of his earlier philandering, debauchery, and cruelty. His later life became marked by atonement, virtue, and spiritual interests. Christian principles became the rule by which he reigned. He was known in his time as "the good king," and was even regarded as an exemplary monarch who embodied biblical standards of admirable sovereignty. Feeling a need for divine support, he requested and received the prayers of his subjects.

Guntram did not pursue virtue determinedly, or at least he wore it with insouciance. To some his moral achievement in his later years was more a matter of simply avoiding vice—say, by refraining from maliciousness and aggression regarding his enemies. Yet he clearly exhibited visibly laudable traits, though perhaps lightheartedly. He has been reported, for example, to have once confronted a treasonous group attempting to kill him with prudence and persuasion rather than might, contending his familial duties and the citizenry's future security simply demanded his longer life and service.

Guntram publicly displayed his faith, though at times in unconventional ways. He was known to refrain occasionally from his usual manner of wearing armor, thereby exposing himself to attack, something he routinely feared. Yet he also proved his devotion not only by frequent attendance at Mass and other services, but also by extended meditation and fasting.[1] The formalized liturgical form of song and prayer known today as the Liturgy of the Hours was celebrated day and night in the chapel of his residence at Chalon.[2]

He encouraged the citizenry, the aristocrats, and even the bishops of his realm to practice virtue as religious persons should. At times he could by his own manner be taken himself for a bishop. His endearment to the church was due to his warm friendships with the episcopacy and other clergy. His concern for discipline among them was evident in the ecclesiastical synods that he encouraged.[3] Without royal pretentiousness he often warmly socialized with priests and bishops, conferring with them and seeking their guidance.[4] They were in fact his primary advisors, especially when

---

1. Gregory of Tours, *History of the Franks*, IX.21.
2. Wood, *Merovingian Kingdoms*, 183.
3. Butler, *Lives*, 1:695–96.
4. Heinzelmann, *Gregory of Tours*, 61, 63, 70, 186–90.

he called them into councils to help solve problems of the kingdom. These relationships served well toward elevating ecclesiastics' esteem of him. He sided with them in decreeing the need for Sunday worship and exhorted them to encourage moral uprightness among the populace of his kingdom. His interests in this regard witnessed to the value of cooperation between civil and ecclesiastical authorities. The bishops respected him not merely because of his royal dignity but also for the piety they saw in him.[5]

His treatment of his subjects were motivated by his sense of justice, which he applied with tenderness.[6] Regarding exploitation as beyond the dictates of virtue and law, he required that any property wrongly confiscated be returned. He attempted with all goodwill to look after his less fortunate subjects by extensively distributing alms and by seeing to the care of the sick. His wealth further served to alleviate the pains of plague and hunger. And he invested in religious practice by founding or endowing many churches and monasteries throughout his realm.

Having reigned for thirty-three years, he died in 593. Scarcely a heartbeat thereafter, his adoring subjects proclaimed him a saint.[7]

SAINT ADELAIDE—MODESTLY MAGNANIMOUS

Captivatingly gorgeous, extremely wealthy, and admirably noble, the talented and productive Adelaide proved to be an invaluable asset to her family, her kingdom, her empire, and her church. Her extraordinary achievements bloomed in tandem with interests and dispositions that were notably spiritual. The characteristics that prompted others to regard her as saintly were multiple and illustrious.

With Adelaide as the inspiration, an air of spirituality and fervor permeated the imperial palace in tenth-century Germany. Such influence had all begun when, with Lothaire as king, she was the young queen of Italy and winning the hearts of her people. Her virtue was apparent and her optimism palpable. Even at nineteen, having just lost her husband of three years, she shared how thankful she was to God for all the good that touched her life and for all the afflictions of which she had been spared.

Her nearly radiant goodness was, beside her renowned physical beauty, something to which King and later Emperor Otto I was attracted when

---

5. Wood, *Merovingian Kingdoms*, 79.
6. Wikipedia, "Guntram," para. 3.
7. Bennett, "Guntramnus," 432–33.

he rescued her from confinement. In marrying her he somewhat reflected her virtue, for he was himself a sovereign of great faith and devoted religious practice.[8] Though domestically and politically astute, Adelaide was a woman of great modesty and devotion. She spent time in fervent prayer. Besides generously sharing her wealth with the needy, she personally offered comfort and compassion for the infirm and hungry. She was devoted to engaging forces of the empire in the work of peace and on behalf of the poor and marginalized. By her directives such goals were to be attained without fanfare, even stealthily.

From her youth she would have been groomed in consciousness of her royal heritage and prestige.[9] But rather than parade the regalia of empress and regent, she directed that materials for such decor be used on behalf of those in need or for liturgical celebration. Throughout her career she was generous in founding, endowing, or restoring monasteries and churches throughout the empire's numerous provinces. She further supported such ecclesiastical institutions with provisions and land.[10]

This, she believed, accorded not only with her faith but also served the needs of the empire. Such values would have been nurtured by her devotion to the Bible, to which she took care to receive instruction from someone eminently qualified. And looking north to the land of Slavs, where she saw nefarious influences of paganism, she did her utmost to facilitate their conversion to Christianity and virtuous living.

Adelaide significantly influenced the culture of medieval Europe with the style of Christianity that she embodied. She had long maintained a close relationship with the abbot of the famous Cluny monastery. She admired him dearly and hoped for divine support through his prayers.[11] It was thus with enthusiasm that she supported the monastery's widespread work of reform in the church.[12]

During the last eight years of her life she made a monastic institution she had founded a kind of retirement home. But this did not exclude her from public engagement. She continued to visit the religious establishments that she supported or revered. Her personal giving to the poor not only did

---

8. Bäumer, *Otto und Adelheid*, 23–25, 35–36.

9. Golinelli, *Adelaide*, 35, 164, 168.

10. Gilsdorf, introduction to *Queenship*, 14.

11. Nash, *Empress Adelheid*, 29–30.

12. Wikipedia, "Adélaïde de Bourgogne," para. 5.

not cease but multiplied.[13] Intent on mediating on behalf of Rudolf, her nephew on the throne of Burgundy, she undertook the task as a charitable mission of peace. Upon return to her retirement community, as the abbey celebrated the anniversary of her son Otto's birth, she was stricken with fever. Consoled by prayer, and comforted by generous intentions on behalf of the poor, she died in 999. On this earth she missed by days the dawn of a new millennium that she and so many others believed would bring the return of Christ. Already recognized by her contemporaries as a saint, she was canonized in 1097 by Pope Urban II.[14]

SAINT HOMOBONUS—OUTSTANDING PRODUCTIVITY AND PASSIONATE CONCERN

He was a big man, both physically and in public life. Running a quite profitable business, he invested not only in trades but in the lives of his twelfth-century compatriots. With his dear wife as a supportive and helpful companion, he brought to his age a new meaning of success. Homobonus worked hard at his trade in Italy's Lombardy, setting the bar high for accomplishment as a wool merchant. His enterprise far exceed that of a small business, and he made enough profit to be able to share it generously with fellow countrymen in need. And he managed to accomplish all of this while maintaining a pleasant home and responsibly supporting family life. By word and example his father had taught him that honesty and integrity were virtues always to be highly regarded and practically exhibited. Dishonesty and injustice thus became abhorrent to Homobonus from his earliest years. Unlike some other merchants of his time who found it hard to be honest, let alone charitable, Homobonus strove to be both, desiring to be a public example of proper business ethics, which in his soul meant remaining visibly committed to his lay status rather than retiring to a monastery. His aspirations succeeded in that he overwhelmingly gained the esteem of his fellow citizens.

From him, other middle-class merchants and artisans would learn that they could retain their wealth in good faith and use it in similar ways. This is noted with some pride by certain "second generation" (thirteenth century) biographers who—unlike their predecessors, and unlike the previous century of church leaders—did not regard the wealth of a rich man

13. Odilo of Cluny, *Epitaph*, 130, 132, 134, 136–39, 141.
14. Golinelli, *Adelaide*, 161–63, 175.

as necessarily a menace to his virtue. He wanted his brand of merchandising to exhibit a kind of spiritual combat against the deeds of the business world. He did not allow his material gain and public recognition to serve self-aggrandizing tendencies in any way.[15] He aspired to profit in order to serve rather than exploit others. This was the opposite of many of his fellow merchants' practices. These entrepreneurs made the poor their victims.[16]

Homobonus however worked tenaciously to sustain the poor. His ethical and spiritual rectitude complemented his attractive physical stature. Some biographers say that he and his wife had accepted their childlessness as God's will. In this case, if such was in fact the case, the disappointment would have left him free for the social and political accomplishments for which he would become famed, a circumstance that blossomed for him into something other than paternal love. Affection for the poor would have become for him a much greater possibility. But the situation of such availability does not necessarily bespeak childlessness as a requisite for intensive philanthropy or charity. For, as we will see, other prosperous and generous saints—and perhaps Homobonus himself—had multiple children, sometimes by more than one spouse after a previous wife's or husband's death. So if, on the other hand, Homobonus had at home several children in his care (the historical data are unclear), the tumultuous hearth could have served as the center of his extended interest, and even energized it.

Charity awakened enthusiasm in him. He felt called by God to see that all the poor of his city could profit from his success in business. He could see it in their faces. Though at times kindly reprimanded by his otherwise adoring wife for his lavish charitable donations from the company's profits,[17] the good man remained silently patient. He generously supported the poor and distributed food to them generously, sometimes to the point of depriving himself of some possession. He even saw to the burial of the impoverished. His surprising and extraordinary ability to provide bread and wine in such quantities to the needy even seemed miraculous to some. He was said not only to have a fatherly attitude toward the poor, but also to be consoling to the sick and those in pain. He visited the needy in their drab settings and spoke to them of spiritual matters. He brought smiles to the faces of ailing children. Even hardened sinners were lead to conversion by his gentle persuasiveness.

15. Butler, *Lives*, 4:334.
16. Bonometti, "Iconografia dimezzata," 23.
17. Wikipedia, "Homobon de Crémone," para. 3.

Living Fully—Godly Energy

When his city of Cremona found itself in the midst of a nearly raging heresy, as a dutiful son of his church he took a firm and decisive stand against fierce opponents of established doctrine but never resorted to violence against them. Here he was not the neutral arbiter but firmly and forthrightly took the official position of his church on what he believed was correct teaching. Such spiritual "warfare" was thought in his times to be as praiseworthy as that of a crusader.[18]

Dedication to daily devotions was for Homobonus a high priority. Habitually sensitive to the divine presence, he was humbly grateful for how God enriched his life. His religious devotion was visible but free of any ostentation.[19] In his later years he adopted a simpler form of dress and frequented less the festivities of high society. Among his exercises of spirituality were his daily attendance at Matins (the predawn prayer of the Divine Office, now called the Liturgy of the Hours) as well as Mass. Repentant before God, he confessed his sins to a Father Oberto, from whom he also received spiritual counsel for twenty-six years. Living out his faith through practical deeds, he truly lived up to the good (*bonus*) resounding in his name. He lived for some eighty years, for fifty of which he was busy at his profession in his exemplary way.[20]

Homobonus appeared as man of great peace and self-mastery.[21] That was the way he appeared as he passed away at Mass in 1197, having fallen on his face, his body in the form of a cross. More than Father Oberto, and more than his wife, the poor of Cremona wept.[22] Homobonus was canonized by Pope Innocent III in 1199,[23] the first lay commoner to be canonized in the Middle Ages. Considering Homobonus's virtue, the ecclesiastical declaration is eminently understandable; but in view of the twelfth-century church leaders' negative view of commercial wealth, canonization of a merchant, let alone a married one, would have required evidence of a heroic saintly life.[24]

---

18. Vauchez, *Omobono*, 19–21, 69–70.
19. Ricci, "Catalogo dei santi," 90.
20. Ricci, "OMOBONO da Cremona," para. 3.
21. Zeno.org, "Homobonus, S," 758.
22. Pedretti, *Sant' Omobono*, 22–24, 29, 33–34, 36–42, 46, 54.
23. Wikipedia, "Saint Homobonus," para. 6.
24. Vauchez, *Omobono*, 35, 57–61.

Good and Wealthy

SAINT ELZÉAR OF SABRAN AND BLESSED DELPHINE OF GLANDÈVES—PASSIONATE VIRGINS

Born into French nobility and later endeared to Italian courts, Elzéar and Delphine were an admirable fourteenth-century couple. Uncommonly chaste in their marriage, they participated with modest pleasure in courtly elegance. As overseers of their households they evoked loyalty and devotion from their servants. The couple's talents and demeanor were not merely the upshot of cultural conditioning but were rooted in profound spirituality. Elzéar had been grounded in his faith by his mother, who also saw to it that virtue duly followed upon his religious belief. Even at a young age he came to appreciate and even enjoy giving attention and assistance to the nearby poor. He also dreamed of being a crusader. His mother's dedication thus facilitated the education and training that he would receive in the monastery from his uncle, the abbot there. The good monk admired the youth's asceticism but had to caution him about excessive austerity. Moderation too is a virtue that must be learned, even by those inclined to sanctity.

Delphine's education under the Abbess of St. Catherine of Sorbo Monastery likewise included formation in virtue. This was apparently no great challenge for the child. Even as a little girl Delphine had found great pleasure in giving alms to the poor who begged at her castle's door. She tried to show them what compassion she could at her age. Her modesty shone too in her reserve regarding compliments for her great beauty. She hardly hungered for notoriety, preferring rather solitude and contemplation. Her home gleamed, framed by the wonder of its natural environment. But she was somewhat indifferent to the grandeur, education, formalities, and grooming enjoyed by the nobility in such a setting. It was not the preferences of such elites that she later found in the abbey, but the realization of her dreams, where prayer and solitude could fruitfully mingle. Her studies there included theology, which she grasped in astounding detail. The vow of virginity, which with Elzéar's affirmation she kept even in marriage, embellished her spiritual life of prayer and generosity toward the poor.

Elzéar's marked propensity for spiritual matters, which include times of fervent prayer that sometimes were ecstatic, allowed him to abstain from prolonged attention to his own needs, even if these were legitimate. Delphine too was drawn to frequent prayer, even during the ceaseless festivities in the castle during the early years of their marriage. Elzéar prayed the Liturgy of the Hours daily, shared prayer with Delphine, and frequently took Communion, a practice in which he found much solace. Thus, while

Living Fully—Godly Energy

loving his wife with profound devotion, he could, replicating her own designs for spirituality and chastity, remain a virgin. Such mutual acceptance of sexual abstinence, while unusual today in the early and middle years of marriages, was embraced by Elzéar as a welcome complement to his spiritual life, especially his dedication to helping those in need. The ancient Greek philosopher Plato, and many theorists of later ages, asserted that the absence of sexual or genital expression in a profound love relationship allowed heightened sensitivity to virtue and the divine. Such attunement to heavenly things could, it was said, be greater than that normally attained by those whose loves involved even appropriate sexuality.

Elzéar's demonstrated care of the poor was consistently accomplished with discretion and humility, without ostentation that sought attention or political gain.[25] Not that he never had second thoughts about the unusual marital arrangement by which he felt freer and energized for charitable service. He even at times voiced his reservations to Delphine. She too occasionally wondered if she was asking too much of him. Yet he consistently remained respectful of her designs, and they both remained faithful to the goals to which they had originally agreed. In later years they would seal their arrangement with formal vows before a priest.

Now and then Elzéar felt the allure of monastic life. Yet he always returned to what he felt in his heart was a divine call to remain engaged in ways of the world in which he had been placed.[26] His enthusiasm for fostering virtue socially was evident in the way he managed the spacious household that they established in Delphine's ancestral home when they both were about twenty. He and Delphine strove to embody what they required of their employees—a worldly engagement resembling monastic life. The servants were to be examples of virtue and relate to others accordingly.[27] All men and women, whether nobles or commoners, were to obey the commandments regarding chastity—namely, all were to refrain from any sexual activity outside of marriage, wherein a man and woman should care for each other lovingly. Decency and reverence in speech were to be maintained at all times. Requisite as well were regular worship and confession. Prayer and charitable works were the order of the day. All, no matter what their rank or social class, were bound by such rules. Clearly the first rule of employment under the devoted couple was to practice virtue. On the job,

---

25. Giangrosso, "Hailigen Ellzearius," 142–43.
26. Bernard, *Époux vierges*, 14–16, 19, 21–22, 42, 44, 58–59, 62–65, 70–74, 132.
27. Donovan, "Blessed Delphine."

integrity must prevail over skill. Needs of the nearby poor were to be met; the hungry should be served, even within the household, and even by the noble couple, who personally visited and helped the sick, relating to them with compassion and tenderness. At the regular organizational meetings, the couple gave expression to their values and invited recommendations; all should listen to one another respectfully; and all were encouraged to mention devotional or spiritual matters.[28]

Later, as the newly designated Lord of Ariano, Elzéar regarded his eventual acceptance by hostile vassals of Naples as evidence of divine assistance.[29] Amid the hustle and bustle of the court, the couple successfully employed the same devoted subterfuge that energized their marital relationship in their previous household. They were cooperative and even contributing participants in all the courtly flourishes; but few knew that behind the scenes their spiritual lives continued to thrive. Harder to hide under the cloak of discretion was their continued service for the poor and sick—there in Italy as it had been in France. Evident too was Elzéar's practice of counseling heartfelt repentance to those sentenced to capital punishment.[30]

It was during his mission to Paris to negotiate the marriage of Naples' Prince Charles that Elzéar became gravely ill. His energies were being typically expended, energetically commingling charitable service with political responsibilities.[31] In the weeks approaching death, his devotion was evident. He received Communion frequently and in his pain listened to stories of Christ's suffering. It was in his last days that he for the first time publicly announced that his marriage with Delphine had been virginal and how she, the good wife that she was, helped him in the pursuit of virtue.[32] Having received Communion for the last time, he died in the arms of his confessor while speaking hopefully of a life beyond. As a lay associate of the Franciscans' religious order, he was clothed in their traditional habit when laid to rest in 1323.[33] He was canonized in 1369 by Pope Urban V.

Delphine lived for thirty-seven more years after Elzéar's death. After King Robert died, his wife, Queen Sanchia, entered a monastery and

---

28. Bernard, *Époux vierges*, 92–94, 98–100.
29. Butler, *Lives*, 3:661.
30. Vauchez, *Laity*, 75.
31. Bernard, *Époux vierges*, 125, 127, 139, 143, 146.
32. Giangrosso, "Hailigen Ellzearius," 145.
33. Carr, "St. Elzéar of Sabran."

LIVING FULLY—GODLY ENERGY

for seventeen years Delphine served as her companion.[34] When the queen died, Delphine returned to France. In her Provençal home she formed a circle of like-minded women with whom she prayed, engaged in household crafts, and discussed spiritual matters, particularly the virtue of chastity. She engaged in occasional penitential exercises, which some criticized as ostentation. For her, however, such practices as begging (a new addition to her asceticism), helping her servants as they worked, and washing their feet were a testimony to her desire for simplicity and charity. Those who knew her well admired her. Many sought her consoling and healing presence. Her final years were marked by suffering, which she bore patiently and without complaint. Before retiring, she had sold all her possessions and given the proceeds to the poor.[35] Thus, as a wealthy person, she followed Jesus' directive to make such a sacrifice (Matt 19:21; Luke 18:22) and replicated what so many others have done in the history of sanctity. Elzéar, like all the other saints whose lives we are following in this book, never took this route, and thus exemplified that self-impoverishment need not be a requisite of exemplary spirituality. Delphine died in 1360. Three years later she was beatified (namely, honored as blessed) ranking her at the stage before full saintly canonization. Devotion to her was widespread. Yet distractions and turmoil in the church precluded further supportive review of her cause, regrettably leaving undetermined when she would be honored with sainthood.[36]

SAINT FERDINAND III—LIFELONG DEVOTION

The astounding life of this model king and conqueror brought medieval Spain honor and prestige throughout Europe. The domain of the Spanish crown was significantly enlarged. Christian culture was restored, expanded, or enhanced in areas that for centuries endured under Islamic sway. Architecture, art, and education thrived. But this was not a story that would facilely unfold. At the age of ten Ferdinand nearly died from a serious illness. One day, stressfully moaning and hearing his mother Berenguela sorrowfully plead with the Virgin Mary for his cure, he clearly realized that he was healed. Many claimed that from a sullen scene had emerged an astounding miracle. The sensitive boy was thereafter drawn

---

34. Pettinati, "Beata Delfina di Signe," para. 4.
35. Donovan, "Blessed Delphine"; Butler, *Lives*, 3:662; Bernard, *Époux vierges*, 218.
36. Wikipedia, "Delphine de Sabran," para. 13.

to frequent prayers to the Virgin, captivated by her influence on his life, and inspired by Berenguela's frequent responses to his queries about his heavenly Mother. Berenguela never remarried after returning to Castile, having separated from León's king. Totally dedicated to her children, she and her devout father, King Alfonso VII, profoundly nurtured the young Ferdinand's religious dispositions.

When Ferdinand, at first with regret, returned to León at the behest of his father, the king, the prince took consolation in extended heartfelt prayer to the mother of his Lord—namely, to Christ's mother Mary. And often, moved more by enthusiasm than grief, he would sing in her honor heartfelt hymns and chants. He would even converse easily with her while riding horseback. At a much younger age he had already assured Berenguela of this firm conviction: by Mary's patronage and intercession he would one day conquer the occupying Muslims, then known in the region as Moors. Heeding his mother's counsel, he also became keenly convinced that virtue and piety would be his greatest strengths as king. Living by such persuasion, he received with gratitude Berenguela's blessing. Later, under the tutelage of his father as a novice knight, the young and bold Ferdinand would, with Mary as an intercessor, adorn his shield the Latin proclamation meaning "God is My Helper." Such fervor would mark his entire kingly and military career.

When Ferdinand was still only fourteen years old, Pope Innocent III proclaimed that the Crusade being launched against the Muslims of the Middle East was being extended into Spain in order to vanquish the Muslim Moors. The ascendancy of Christendom in Spain, the *reconquista* of the land by the Christian faithful, began quickly and successfully with the 1212 battle at Navas. And Ferdinand, upon hearing of it, vowed to be part of a complete victory in the rest of the land. His devotion intensified. He attended Mass daily and prayed fervently to become a courageous knight in the Lord's army. He could recite in Latin long prayers and blessings from the Bible or from the Liturgy of the Hours, known then as the Divine Office. Ferdinand was quite subject to anger and could feel it intensely at times. His efforts to control it only came to full fruition when, following biblical guidance, he would forgive the person who was the object of his anger. Such serenity was the source of his otherwise nearly habitual state of joy.

The deep Christian faith by which Ferdinand strove to live compelled him as well to motivate others in their own self-betterment. He encouraged devotion in his children and helped with instructing them in their faith.[37] When he suggested that one of his daughters become a nun, she lovingly and enthusiastically complied. The several times he left the magnificence of his castle to visit her, he was captivated in a deeply spiritual way by the poverty and simplicity in which she lived. Monastic vows were decidedly alluring. He firmly professed however that what he had been given in life was by divine decree and that he had to remain true to the lay and kingly calling enjoined on him by God.

Throughout his life he frequently complemented his daily prayer with devotional fasting. Jesus' mother, Mary, remained particularly dear to Ferdinand and an unrelenting object of his devotion. On the front of his saddle a statue of her was mounted prominently, soaring ahead of him as he charged into battles on his great white horse. He had in his earlier years thoroughly familiarized himself with his predecessors' military tactics. He had diligently practiced in the effective use of weapons, and drilled in horsemanship under challenging conditions. After his adolescence he attained a muscular build that served him well in battle. Nonetheless he credited his military victories, and his kingship itself, to Mary's Son, the Lord to whom he continually turned with thankfulness. Ferdinand's marked though humble religiousness was so evident that the citizenry of his kingdom called him "the saint."

His attention to the poor was notorious. Even in his teens, while living with his father in León, the prince would stand at the door of the castle church, generously and affectionately distributing alms. Once an impoverished woman, impressed by his good looks, humility, and generosity, evoked a blessing on him and his future reign. He in turn believed that the humble poor would be a great asset to his royal domain. Even at his wedding feast he generously made sure that the impoverished nearby could amply partake of the food and celebration. During his reign his attendants in Castile would daily feed from the castle's stock any of the destitute appearing at the door. Often Ferdinand himself would help prepare and serve the meals. One Holy Thursday, emulating Christ's tenderness at the Last Supper, he selected twelve of the impoverished and humbly washed their feet.

Ferdinand's eminent desire that his subjects live uprightly was inspired by his conviction that their virtue was the deepest root of what happiness they enjoyed, even as he worked to ameliorate their conditions materially.

---

37. Fitzhenry, *Saint Fernando III*, 229.

In the pursuit of such happiness or blessedness, he joined the Franciscans' Third Order, a group of laity dedicated to the ascetical practices of St. Francis of Assisi. He attested publicly to his own shortcomings or sins. To facilitate the spiritual formation of his subjects he oversaw the widespread renewal of Catholic devotion and liturgy. To this end he welcomed to Spain the Dominicans, Franciscans, and Trinitarians—newly founded religious orders.

His loyalty to the church and its directives was evident in many ways. Among the loftiest of Ferdinand's goals was facilitation in spreading his Christian faith. At his coronation he prayerfully professed his desire to spread faith in the cross of Christ. Thus Ferdinand's asceticism was particularly intense before battles, which for him were not mere warring conquests but achievements honoring his God and faith. The discipline he sought in his warriors was more of a spiritual than physical nature. They had to be forceful and skillful with weapons of war but even stronger in virtues—the admirable dispositions of character and faith that brought vibrancy and valor were not characteristic of physical prowess alone. His Franciscan and Dominican chaplains fervently assisted in exhorting his armies to such strengths.[38]

Not that Ferdinand's faith never faced trials. One of the greatest was during the tremendously difficult siege of Seville, when scorching heat and fever brought death to some of his finest fellow warriors. Ravaged by doubt and close to despair, he nonetheless held fast to belief in the God from whom he was feeling no consolation. Aware of the darkness in which the king was struggling, his loving and sensitive wife, Queen Joan, who as usual was encamped nearby, commissioned that an exceptionally beautiful statue of the Virgin Mary be crafted for him. On seeing it and confessing that his doubts were being sown by the devil, he gradually found consolation and a renewed sense of victory.

His belief in the church as the leaven of Spanish and European culture led him to vigorously support the church's opposition to Albigensianism. This thirteen-century form of ancient Gnosticism professed that the enduring powers of darkness were in such a permanent struggle against divinely initiated goodness that not even the power of redemption could undo it. Their extremist adversity to established institutions made them a threat to civic order and many religious practices. Ferdinand was always ready to treat with leniency the repentant among them. But his unflinching

38. Beretz, "Ferdinand III of Castile."

Living Fully—Godly Energy

Christian faith with its optimism based on divine intervention on behalf of humanity and creation led him to forthrightly resist the Albigensian view that his church called a heresy. Such spiritual warfare naturally complemented his prowess in physical battle.

In 1252 he was struck with such a serious and rapidly advancing illness that he realized his end was near. He had apparently planned to extend his military campaigns into North Africa. An initially successful venture to Morocco won some benefits for Christians there.[39] But he accepted his affliction as a sign that continued expansion was not to be the case.[40] Having spent a life of accomplishment, renown, and notable integrity, he approached death with humility, reverence, and repentance. When the viaticum—Communion to accompany him beyond this life—was brought to him, he insisted on receiving it on his knees, despite intense afflictions.

Having returned to his bed, he exhorted his son Alfonso, who would soon be king of Castile and León, to seek success by fearing, loving, and obeying God, always fulfilling the divine will. Thus, said the king, Alfonso would find salvation. Finally, he enjoined upon Alfonso the task of codifying the nation's laws so that the entire citizenry could be justly governed consistently.[41]

He desired to be buried not robed as a nobleman or king but as one dedicated to virtue. His final words bear witness to his intense faith: "I came naked, Lord, from the bosom of my mother, the earth, to whom I now naked offer myself; receive me, Lord, into the company of your servants."[42] And so it was. In 1252, having exhorted his oldest son to use his incomparable wealth favorably as a good king should,[43] and adorned solely in the simple robe of the Franciscan Third Order, Ferdinand was laid to rest in the Sevillian cathedral. His tomb—remarkably inscribed in Castilian Spanish, Latin, Hebrew, and Arabic—evidenced what widespread respect he had attained among Christians, Jews, and Muslims.[44] He was suitably placed near an image of the Virgin for whom the inspiring edifice was named. Over the centuries this morally edifying and model Christian leader was hardly

---

39. Laurentie, *Saint Ferdinand*, 169–71, 175.

40. Fitzhenry, *Saint Fernando III*, 15, 95–97, 104, 106, 308–13, 328–29.

41. Fernández, *King of Castile*, xi, 2–9, 16–19, 21, 24, 26–27, 37–39, 44, 62, 78, 195–97, 275.

42. Maccono, *Ferdinando III*, 225.

43. Maccono, *Ferdinando III*, 57–58, 225.

44. Ballan, "Tomb of Fredinand III," para. 4.

forgotten, as numerous acts of devotion at his resting place attested. Pope Clement X canonized him in 1671.[45]

SAINT MARGARET OF SCOTLAND—INFECTIOUS SPIRITUALITY

The young English lady eventually left her homeland under duress, only to finally adopt Scotland as her new domain. Having married its king, Malcolm, she endeared herself to the court and the Scottish people. Her innovations brought new color and luster to the trappings and architecture of the palace and its grounds. She helped the eleventh-century nation as a whole profit by enhanced trade. And by her influence the church saw reorganization that brought it new life. Margaret was a woman of enduring virtue, honorable conduct, and admirable nobility. She spoke with wisdom that flowed from virtue and meditative insight. Contemporaries regarded her as exemplarily devoted to her religion.[46] To her earliest biographers she was truly a "pearl," as suggested even by her name, Margaret, which is derived from the Greek word for that jewel of the sea.

She therefore reflected well the influence of her mother, Agatha, whose virtue proved her a renowned and admirable member of the Hungarian royal court, which had been converted to Christianity through the leadership of the king, who would come to be known as Saint Stephen of Hungary. The conduct of the court reflected its religious heritage, and the young Margaret grew up well instructed in the elements of her faith. In a Christian environment still threatened by paganism, she could well become imbued with an unflinching trust in an omnipotent God.

Margaret was well educated, literate in both English and Latin. As an adolescent in England, she had already begun to read and enjoy spiritual and theological works of such greats as St. Augustine and St. Benedict. Thus the allure of the vibrant secular world surrounding her paled, significantly enhancing her attraction to a more contemplative way of life.

Though later in Scotland she valued her luxurious lifestyle and stately dress, she did not exorbitantly cling to them. She regarded them as emblems of royal stature and duty. So her character reflected modesty and humility.[47] She felt that all that she materially possessed and enjoyed should

---

45. Heckmann, "St. Ferdinand III," 6.
46. Butler, *Lives*, 3:517.
47. Turgot, *Vita Margaretae*, 153.

Living Fully—Godly Energy

be used for God's purposes, especially for the needs of others. The young queen led a life of exceptional piety, with regular devotion to prayer. She attended to her spiritual life discreetly however, always dutifully aware of what was rightly expected of her as queen. She was careful to avoid fault and always welcomed forthright criticism. Her greatest failure was to have fasted excessively, thus weakening herself and disposing herself to illness.

She felt it was God's will that she marry King Malcolm, attracted more to the spiritual value of the new relationship than to either the royal glamour that accompanied it or even the monastically virginal life to which she was once attracted.[48] Midnight attendance at prayers of the Divine Office was her daily practice, frequently costing her needed sleep. Such veneration was not lost on her husband, the king, who often accompanied her to that devotion's nocturnal vigils. Her lively spiritual disposition and practice were highly influenced by the Rule of St. Benedict, a work her Benedictine educators had introduced to her early on and one she came to treasure. So she strove consistently to be patient and forgiving, to remember others in prayer, including the dead, and to be for others a balm of compassion and source of counsel.

Though familiar with and duly welcoming royal mannerisms, in her daily life she mostly ate modestly and dressed simply. She read the Bible regularly for edification and understanding. The Four Gospels were especially dear to her. When unsure how to interpret Scripture, she sought the counsel of competent scholars, though it was often they who went away the wiser.[49] Her reverence for the Bible edified her husband King Malcolm, who spoke Scotch, English, and Latin but could not read. He profited greatly from her scriptural readings as well as from the example of her virtuous life. This was eminently evident in the admirable aspects of his reign. Margaret helped turn a rough and unrefined master of the court into one of the most polished, cultured, and virtuous Scottish kings.[50] Together they strove for justice, sincere and practical religiosity, and widespread contentment in their kingdom.

Malcolm was so impressed by Margaret's faith that he respected her perspective on all matters, not only within the royal palace but also regarding matters of state. That respect did not attenuate however the strain of

---

48. Menzies, *St. Margaret*, 6–12, 20, 42, 45, 53–54, 65, 152, 155; Keene, *Saint Margaret*, 41.

49. Turgot, *Dunfermline Vita*, 178, 183.

50. Butler, *Lives*, 3:515.

ferocity invariably characterizing his dispositions toward England. Margaret's influence had its limits.

Her pious dispositions influenced the character of each of her children. This was especially so regarding the Scottish prince and future king, David, who would himself in later times be named a saint. Good and loving parents nurture in the souls of their young the seeds of virtue that otherwise remain woefully dormant. A child may be born to be greatly magnanimous but must be encouraged to attain it. Margaret personally instructed her little ones in the faith and oversaw their education, though caretakers also gave them considerable time. The children were to love God above all. She taught them to abhor immoral behavior and indecent language at all costs. They were to display the greatest reverence toward God and Mary, the mother of Jesus. Heeding Jesus' words, she made clear, was a sure path to lasting joy and whatever prosperity accompanied it. Her great desire was that her children learn that prosperity should never be a distraction from spiritual pursuits.[51] So she wanted all her young to be generous and loving toward the poor, particularly attending to the protection of orphans. It was eminently important, she taught, to associate only with virtuous persons and heed their advice. Overall, she showed her children how to be steadfast in the practice of their faith. Their caretakers were quite aware of the queen's directives and were expected to heed them diligently and strictly. The royal children thus appeared to all as mannerly, wholesome in their upbringing, and reverent. As adults they were known for their piety and generosity and achieved much that benefitted the church and Scottish society.

To enhance the worshipful atmosphere of the royal residence and its grounds, she had the palace church extensively enlarged and sumptuously decorated with silver, gold, and precious stones. She had the church rededicated and staffed with monks of the Benedictine order. This was one of her first major achievements after assuming queenship.

Her days abounded in works of charity. Jesus' gospel exhortation that the just believer serve him by serving others was for her a most serious rule.[52] She treated her servants with great kindness and notably expanded the royal household to include twenty-four elderly citizens as advisers, whom she supported through all their remaining years. When traveling from the palace, flocks of the poor and needy surrounded her and were inspired by her attention. She visited the sick and helped care for them personally. She

---

51. Turgot, *Dunfermline Vita*, 212.
52. Dunlop, *Queen Margaret of Scotland*, 20, 28–29, 49, 51–52, 55–57.

Living Fully—Godly Energy

displayed exceptional generosity in giving alms. Sometimes when her own immediate funds were depleted by such generosity, she would borrow from attendants at the royal court, who willingly gave, knowing they would be repaid in full or with interest. King Malcolm reacted similarly to the destiny of some of his private funds, laughing off that she tried to borrow from him surreptitiously, while he facetiously but lovingly threatened to have her imprisoned for theft. When Englishmen captured by the Normans were brought to Scotland as serfs, Margaret had their cases examined and paid the ransoms of those particularly aggrieved.

Prior to her own breakfast she sought daily to assuage the hunger of nearby orphans and those struck by poverty. Typical was the grateful presence of nine tiny beggars, whom she often held and fed personally. To many hundreds of the poor she regularly opened the great dining hall of the palace and helped feed the guests herself. Often she extended to beggars, or to pilgrims at the nearby shrine, the extraordinary service of washing their feet in emulation of Jesus.[53] In all of this Malcolm dutifully and reverently assisted her.[54]

The queen built hostels for travelers. Among the many ecclesiastical institutions that she founded was the famous majestic Abbey of Dunfermline, where she and other royalty would eventually be buried.[55] The abbey was built for Benedictine monks to enshrine a relic dear to Margaret, a wooden remnant said to be a portion of Jesus' cross. Margaret facilitated pilgrimages to the shrine by establishing two ferries for easy access to it. She also saw to it that appropriate personnel would serve the pilgrims' needs. A nearby cave functioned as a retreat for her where she would pray. On one occasion, Malcolm, finding her there, was impressed and humbled by her devotion. So he decided to have the cave properly furnished to accommodate her devotions.[56]

In 1093, at the age of forty-eight, she lay in illness while grieving the loss of both her husband and oldest son in a battle with the English. Her surviving son Edgar had compassionately given her the sad news. Close to death, she did not despair. She was holding a beautiful cross that was particularly dear to her.[57] Among her final words were ones that attest to her

---

53. Marshall, "Malcolm Canmore"; Keene, *Saint Margaret*, 73.
54. McRoberts, *Margaret Queen of Scotland*, sec. 2, para. 5.
55. Hunter-Blair, "Abbey of Dunfermline."
56. Keene, *Saint Margaret*, 74.
57. Turgot, *Dunfermline Vita*, 202, 216.

profound sense of loss but mostly to her unbounded hope: "I thank thee, Almighty God, that in sending me so great an affliction in the last hour of my life, thou wouldst purify me from my sins, as I hope, by thy mercy."[58] In peace she passed away. Yet the memory of her holiness, charity, and dedication to the church lived on. Pope Innocent IV canonized her in 1250.[59]

SAINT LOUIS IX—LOVER OF VIRTUE

Louis was a king to whom the eyes of thirteenth-century Europe avidly turned. Here was a French noble, lavish in lifestyle, enamored and productive in marriage, dedicated to religion and the arts, and intent on justice for all in his domain. As a youth his religious education was a heartfelt concern of his mother, Blanche; the boy should love God; and, though a prince, he should revere his baptism more than his royal status. These foremost principles she instilled in him personally. Her motherly guiding hand was like a sweet breeze of spring upon a gently awakening bud. Louis was also to accompany her every day to the communally prayed Divine Office. She influenced his associations too, limiting them to church personnel or those closely aligned with the royal family's Christian religion.

Ever mindful of his devout mother's declaration that she preferred his death to his committing mortal sin, his later life was marked by exemplary devotion and good works. Ever hungry for inspiration, he enjoyed listening to sermons. Chaplains were a standard part of his retinue, and he often invited prominent preachers of the day, such as the Franciscan St. Bonaventure, to expound on the gospels. It was his habit to spend extended time in prayer, convinced that his duty was to pray more for his people than for himself. He often prayed alone in his room, with solemnity but without fanfare, though attendants were often nearby. His daily participation in public liturgies, such as the Divine Office and Mass, was remarkable for its serenity and profound devotion. For him prayer was not simply the recitation of religious formulas or pious words but essentially the expression of profound sentiments by which, he deeply believed, he related to God.[60] Prayer flowed from his heart like a bounteous spring. He fasted regularly,

---

58. Butler, *Lives*, 3:517.

59. Menzies, *St. Margaret*, 60–61, 108–13, 119–21, 130–31, 175–76, 180–81; Wikipedia, "Saint Margaret of Scotland," para. 17.

60. Le Goff, "Louis et la prière," 1, 86, 89.

Living Fully—Godly Energy

especially during holy seasons, and at other times ate modestly as an act of penance and humility.

Louis encouraged his children to join him in attendance at Mass, in chanting the Divine Office, and in listening to sermons. He prayed with the children regularly, and before bedtime sang with them a hymn to the Virgin Mary.

His series of admonitions to his oldest son, Philip, began with an admonition to love God with a fervent heart. This meant above all to obey God, steadfastly submitting to divine imperatives and humbly accepting success as attributable to God. Heartfelt and prayerful submission to the word of God was the foundational principle of all the admonitions.[61] Reverence for the holy word prompted Louis to order the first French translation of the Bible.[62]

Louis practiced self-denial, especially during Lent when he wore an uncomfortable hair-cloth belt next to his skin. Such practices evidenced the king's profound and ongoing sense that he was blessed with a relationship to God and must then faithfully and meticulously do all that he felt God was asking of him, always ready, if need be, to set a new course.[63] To remain steadfast in the life of faith, he told his son Philip, one should wholeheartedly pray to God, especially at Mass during the consecration of the bread and wine. This son, so dear to him, should therefore be penitent, loyal to the church, generous to the poor, always open to religious admonitions, temperate in speech and action, dedicated to peace making, and careful in selecting good and diligent administrators. Louis was thus exemplary in demonstrating that a king's advancement in virtue was accomplished through the rightful, noble, and pious exercise of royalty. When reprimanded by others for his generosity, Louis replied that he preferred spiritually motivated almsgiving to pompous worldly extravagance. He was convinced that as both as king and as a Christian, his expression of faith should be exemplary, modeling for his people what eminently favored the good of France.

As to wealth the king exhorted Philip to thank God humbly for whatever prosperity may come from divine providence, for this enfeebles the self-assuring pride that alienates one from God and disposes one to worthily receive any other gifts from heaven. Moreover, if competent investigators

---

61. Cantor, *Middle Ages*, 450.
62. See Wikipedia, "Ludwig IX. (Frankreich)," sec. "Ludwig der Heilige als Christ."
63. Gaposchkin, *Making Saint Louis*, 190.

should determine that some possession has been acquired unduly, prompt restitution should be made.

Convinced that the poor were channels of justice and peace in his kingdom, he fed them and gave them coin of the realm, thus attending with sincerity and devotion to many of his impoverished subjects. Such action toward the destitute was replicated by Louis multiple times in various settings far from his castle. Thus he exhorted his son to likewise show compassion to the poor and miserable to the extent that it was within royal power.[64] Such compassion had been evident even in Louis's childhood. Later as king he consciously emulated Jesus' washing his disciples' feet, literally washing the feet of beggars and serving them from his table; he took his own sustenance from scraps of the more than one hundred poor who ate in his home daily. At times he would personally cut the food of the very sick and feed them with his own hand.[65] His household included someone whose specific task it was to distribute money and clothing to the impoverished. Sometimes he himself would go out from the palace alone on horseback under the cover of night to secretly and without recognition give money to the poor of the streets.[66] Louis also cared for the sick by meeting the needs of lepers and by establishing hospitals and homes for the ailing, the blind, and former prostitutes. One of his hospitals contained a chapel for worship. For the first time ever, governmental projects helped support the destitute or deprived—assistance heretofore had only been provided by the church or private individuals.

The Cistercian abbey which he helped to build at Royaumont was often for him a place of spiritual retreat. The companionship he shared with the monks was lively, freshened by spiritual air. With them the king would pray, chant in choir, share meals, and take particular interest in their care of lepers in their infirmary. Though a man of faith and devotion, Louis avoided theological disputes, thinking such should be reserved for the clergy educated in such matters.[67]

After an illness in 1248 he was inspired to participate in a Crusade in defense of Christians pilgrims to the Holy Land. They were being ravished by sophisticated Muslim armies. Louis apparently believed he could help to deter them. But more importantly he was intent on facilitating

---

64. de Joinville, *Life of St. Louis*, 214–15.
65. Le Goff, *Saint Louis*, 498–500, 505–7, 603–4, 610, 630–31.
66. Folz, *Saints roi*, 109, 151.
67. Richard, *St. Louis*, 76, 78–79, 238, 240–41.

Living Fully—Godly Energy

their conversion. His army enjoyed some success. Since the king was less interested in killing and more interested in taking Muslims as prisoners (especially the women and children), some Muslims did convert; and Louis eventually brought many of them back to France. Yet the mission was for the most part futile militarily.

During the campaign Louis had been captured in Egypt, leaving his wife, Marguerite, in charge of his army,[68] a strategy signaling both her competence and his confidence in her. During his captivity he continued his recitation of the Divine Office, as had always been his daily practice, whether participating in the readings and prayers communally or reciting them privately. His piety nurtured an honesty so unabated that he staunchly resisted any suggestion of cheating his Muslim captors out of any of the ransom promised to them for his release. In a famous meeting with the Muslim sultan who had captured him, but who politely addressed him as "lord king," Louis solemnly admitted that his greatest sense of loss was in not having seen more Muslims converted.

After being set free for a sizeable sum quickly collected by Marguerite, he visited and financially supported the recently established Crusader states in the Middle East; there he visited many of the holy places and worked to foster diplomatic relations with some Islamic leaders in the area. During his journey home, Louis and his fellow voyagers survived a violent and dangerous storm at sea. The king took their safety as a divine sign challenging him to a renewed and more profound practice of his faith.

Upon his return to France, he adopted a simpler lifestyle manifested in his manner and dress. Royal garments yielded their silk to broadcloth, and the royal bed yielded its feathers to cotton. The king increasingly felt the need to serve as a moral and spiritual exemplar for his people. Simplicity in sovereignty did not however bring obscurity. The kindness and generosity of this ideal Christian gentleman shined bright. His renown in France was amplified by emulation throughout Europe, a distinction not common among most of the continent's other rulers.

Though in ill health, during his final days his compassion for the beleaguered Christians in the Middle East impelled him to launch another Crusade, accompanied in the usual manner by chaplains of the Trinitarian order. He died in Tunis however with, as one chronicler reports, the words of Jesus on his lips: "Into your hands I commend my spirit" (Luke 23:46).[69]

---

68. See Wikipedia, "Louis IX," sec. "Échec Final."
69. Richard, *St. Louis*, 76, 78–79, 147, 151, 238–41, 326.

By another account, his final movements found him humbly praying for his people and confidently hoping for eternal life.[70]

Thus ended the edifying life of a saint who prodigiously enhanced the French throne's prestige. An inspiration to all who knew him, he was canonized by Pope Boniface VII in 1297, just twenty-seven years after his death in 1270.[71] The pope's sermon on that memorable occasion made allusion to Ephesians 3:38, "I pray that you may have the power to comprehend, with all the saints, what is the breadth and length and height and depth . . ." For Boniface regarded Louis as "long in perseverance, wide in his charity, deep in his humility, and high . . . in his right intention toward God."[72]

VENERABLE PIERRE TOUSSAINT—PROPAGATOR OF GOOD CHEER

He was a prominent hairdresser in New York City while several of America's first presidents served, during the decades before and after the end of the eighteenth century. And he enjoyed notorious financial success. His prominence however was due at least as much to his refinement and virtue as to his skill. Pierre grew up as a privileged black slave in a St. Domingan environment where his grandmother, mother, and master lived their faith with clear devotion. Unlike liaisons among many of the island's colonial elite, relationships of all in the household were morally exemplary. Having been baptized in accord with his master's wishes, he learned much more about his beliefs—mostly, it would seem, in the master's library, where he could read the works of famous French preachers and memorize many passages.

His own spiritual bearing throughout his life was clear. Part of his daily routine in New York was praying Matins or the Office of Readings (part of the Divine Office), and attending early morning Mass. He regularly read the Bible and emulated its heroes. His book of prayers was always with him, and he often quoted from the classic tractate *The Imitation of Christ*.

Though by his own admission his temper was volatile, he was quick to forgive anyone who offended him. His charitableness was markedly evident in his joy at providing cheer for others. His St. Domingan aunt was part of his widowed putative owner's New York household. When she became increasingly plagued by gloom and withdrawal, he strove to hearten her

---

70. Le Goff, *Saint Louis*, 81–82, 111, 226, 624, 646–50, 667–70.

71. Goyau, "St. Louis IX,"; Wikipedia, "Louis IX of France," para. 33.

72. Gaposchkin, "Sanctity of Louis IX," 25–26.

Living Fully—Godly Energy

with fashionable coiffures. Later the householder herself became heartsick. Like many of her compatriots, she was disillusioned by Napoleon's failure to restore St. Domingo's economy after the slaves there rebelled and the household had to flee to New York. Pierre strove to lift her spirits with gifts and flowers. At times he arranged and financed for her delight colorful parties where he served as waiter and musician. When remarriage alleviated her gloom but made her financially burdened by her new husband's unavoidable insolvency, Pierre once again, from his independent wealth, generously presented himself as the household's mainstay, and he did so with no expectation of repayment.

Totally aside from these commitments, his assistance to others became so well known that appeals for his support significantly increased. And he responded, irrespective of the supplicant's status or the color of their skin.[73] He provided the impoverished with household items. He supported priests in their mission work, seminarians in their studies, and immigrants in bringing their families from abroad. His motivation, like that for his lifelong charitable work, was highly spiritual, rooted in his belief in an encouraging heavenly Father, and thus in the familial solidarity of all on earth. His refined theology translated into practical spirituality.

He stood loyally by his owner as she lay dying and called a priest to bless her final moments. The financial burden of caring for her had forced him to postpone marriage to Juliette Noel, despite his ever-deepening love for her. Having eventually married her, they turned their apartment into a warm and welcoming resource for many variously in need. The lively Juliette shared Pierre's generous disposition. Many in want, white or black, received from them comfort, both physical and emotional. The couple's care for them was heartfelt and steadfast. On a wall hung a crucifix given to Pierre in gratitude by a priest he had helped. Orphans, refugees, beleaguered travelers and the abandoned learned that they could rely on him for shelter, loans, emotional support, or assistance in finding work.

Juliette became pregnant more than once, but never bore children. The Toussaint couple did adopt their orphaned niece, a sickly child for whom they cared lovingly. The series of homeless black youths that they fostered were sheltered until Pierre could find employment for them, sometimes training them himself in specialized skills. He hired one of these lads as his own apprentice and another as his errand runner. Others he readied for civilian tasks supporting military preparations for a possible invasion

---

73. Sheehan and Odell, *Pierre Toussaint*, 35, 84–86.

by the British during the War of 1812. The charity of the Toussaint couple sprang from a natural disposition supported by their spiritual sense of responsibility.

Pierre helped to finance the rebuilding of the New York parish church that he regularly attended. When funds were solicited to build a new church for French immigrants, he was among the first donors. He guided his wealthy Catholic and Protestant clients in founding an orphanage for the many youth left parentless because of New York's then devastatingly germ-ridden environment. His forty years of financial support for the home provided just one example of his prominent monetary generosity.

Such giving was matched by his personal assistance to those in need. He would go into sections of the city plagued by yellow fever to nurse the sick and dying. His innate empathy made him an adept counselor skilled in supporting the afflicted, especially the bereaved, whether by comforting words or reverential silence. The spacious house that he and Juliette eventually acquired included a small chapel-like area where Pierre prayed. At times Pierre brought into the house some of the sick and nursed them there. As in all such cases, he did so gratuitously.

His faith was sorely tested as he was crushed by the death of the dear teenage niece he had helped to raise. He even appeared to be mortally wounded by the emotional pain. With Juliette's encouragement and the prayerful support of friends, he returned with vigor to his professional, charitable, and compassionate ways. His sorrows had rendered him even more sensitive to need. When someone wondered why he did not retire but continued to work so hard at accruing profit when he already was prosperous enough to retire, he kindly responded that others would thereby be neglected.

With his gift for providing wise counsel, he was revered by many of his clients as a trusted confidant. His virtues and devotion were so widely evident that he was spoken of as holy even in his own lifetime. One of his clients regarded him as her personal "saint." By such esteem he was indeed the saint of New York City. On one occasion however an insensitive usher refused to admit him, Juliette, and their guest to New York's original cathedral, which Pierre had helped to finance. Pierre reacted with muted dignity, acquiescing judiciously, as he sometimes did, to prevailing white prejudice. The incident elicited a prolonged heartfelt apology from the cathedral's trustees and provoked widespread shock and embarrassment in the circles where he was so admired.[74]

Pierre's sanctity was evident as a fine complement to his gifts as a teacher. By simple words and gentle example he led some to faith. Moreover he was uncommonly informed theologically, having continued from childhood the practice of studying and memorizing scholarly treatises. His lucid explanations of church teachings on such matters as Marian devotion and sacramentality brought him honor and admiration from both Protestants and Catholics. Eloquence and affability, along with pride in being black, helped him as well to mitigate racial prejudice. He supported black educators and with Juliette helped establish for young blacks the city's first Catholic school.

Juliette's death left him grief-stricken and desolate. They had for decades thrived in wondrous marital partnership. As his pace slowed, illness brought his final days, which he embraced with his usual gentlemanly manner, comforted by Communion and the visits of friends.[75] Desiring nothing more "on earth," he died in 1856 at approximately the age of eighty (the exact date is disputed)[76] having earned widespread respect for his warmth and benevolence. Thus lavish praise marked local newspapers' extended coverage of his passing. At his exquisite and solemn funeral the presiding priest declared that Pierre was among the foremost of all those who by their lives gave glory to God.[77] In 1997 he was solemnly designated as venerable,[78] thus formally elevating him to the first step in the Vatican's process of officially naming him a saint.

BLESSED FRÉDÉRIC OZANAM— A COUNTERCULTURAL ADVOCATE FOR JUSTICE

He was a lad whose parents taught him to respond to the needs of the poor. He was an enthusiastic student who burned with desire to turn theory into action. He was a renowned professor who found practicable truths in classical art and poetry. He was a dedicated citizen who exercised responsible

---

74. Tarry, *Pierre Toussaint*, 202–3, 297, 300–302, 314–20.

75. Lee, *Memoir of Pierre Toussaint*, 23–24, 36–37, 48–49, 56, 70–71, 81, 102, 105, 112.

76. Jones, *Pierre Toussaint*, 37–39, 49, 171, 177, 214, 226, 269–70, 313–16.

77. Hanley, "Pierre Toussaint," para. 95.

78. African American Registry, "Pierre Toussaint," para. 9.

citizenship in extraordinary ways. For all of that he was a nineteenth-century gentleman and a man of honor. But he was more.

At the age of six the young Frenchman Frédéric Ozanam nearly died of typhoid fever. This was the beginning of a lifelong struggle with illnesses. It was said that his recovery from the early fever came through the healing hand of St. John Francis Regis, who had generously served the poor of France nearly two centuries earlier. Late in life Frédéric recalled that his mother had prayed for the saint's intercession.[79] She was a woman of deep spiritual devotion[80] and fostered in Frédéric a strong religious disposition. His dedication to his faith was remarkably evident in the reverence with which he made his First Communion at the age of thirteen. But living in what appeared to him as a powerful and disturbing secular milieu, at fifteen he experienced painful doubts about religion. Frédéric nonetheless vowed that he would spend his life defending whatever divine truth he might find. Only a year later, with the support of a teacher, he began to publish articles in support of his faith. The turnaround was not just theoretical but was enlivened by his desire to strive conscientiously for virtue. His writings were very well received and his character greatly admired.[81] But shortly thereafter, while studying law in Paris, he found himself encountering once more a disheartening secular and starkly anti-Christian atmosphere. The challenge to remediate such spiritual desolation tugged on his speculative mind. Again he received encouragement, this time from a learned man who was a well-known scientist. Frédéric's reflections led to his founding the Conference of Charity, with beneficence as a hallmark.

Frédéric's religious sensitivity was profound and rich. After rediscovering his faith in his late teens, he nurtured his belief though enjoyment of nature. Its colors and contours awakened a sense of wonder by which he gave thanks to God. Life's material comforts were hardly comparable to this, or to the inspiration of art and poetic imagery. Nature and artistry were the partners of his devotional exercises. Daily prayer, pondering biblical passages for half an hour a day, frequent attendance at Mass, devotion to Mary and other saints, and spiritual reading became part of young Frédéric's regular routine, and remained so for the rest of his life. As a teacher and laborer for the poor he profoundly entrusted his work to

---

79. Bernardelli, *Storia*, 131.
80. Scott, "Frédéric Ozanam," 34.
81. Rybolt, "Virtuous Personality," 36–37.

Living Fully—Godly Energy

divine providence. Though he occasionally experienced disturbing times of spiritual desolation,[82] his faith grew in practical ways.

He believed deeply that his marriage to Amélie, and the birth of their daughter Marie, were designed by God. Holding the little girl he could sense a divinely created soul, a flower destined for eternity.[83] By the age of five she was sweetly imitating her parents in prayer.[84] Their example was visibly edifying. Though attentive to income and spending—Amélie more so—they both agreed that their happiness was rooted in their marriage, not in money. Throughout their life together they prayed for one another regularly.[85] Frédéric felt blessed to live comfortably but not opulently, to thus be better positioned to exhort those of greater means to greater charity and those of lesser means to the kind of grateful receptivity that allows for the dissolution of antipathies and the nurturing of friendly mutuality, whereby the gap between the rich and the poor could be minimized as much as practically possible.[86]

During his later professorial years, after the Conference of Charity of his student years expanded exponentially into the Society of St. Vincent de Paul, he and his partners labored all the more intently to bring help to those in need. In 1848 the French government called on Frédéric and the society to provide relief for the many left impoverished after some workers' insurrection. Later the society's generosity was called upon to care for two thousand Parisians afflicted by an epidemic of cholera.

Compassion for the poor of such locales as Paris, where he spent years, and London, which he briefly visited, was typical of Frédéric's dedication and tenderness throughout his student and adult life. Knowing of his kindness, the poor would frequently seek him out at home, and he received them courteously, even if he was busy with his books and writing. Once he was annoyed by a recidivate beggar but quickly apologized for impatience with him. For, in Frédéric's words, sentiments toward the poor should always be that "you are the visible image of the God whom we do not see, but whom we love in loving you."[87] In other words, serving the poor was

---

82. Sickinger, *Antoine Frédéric Ozanam*, 17, 198–99, 202; Baunard, *His Correspondence*, 342.

83. Bernardelli, *Storia*, 68.

84. Cholvy, *Christianisme a besoin*, 215, 217, 223, 229–30.

85. Harrison, *Romantic Catholics*, 214.

86. Ozanam, *Letters*, 91–92, 106.

87. Mercier, "Ozanam et la misère," 56.

not for Frédéric merely an admirable deed but more meaningfully a sacred action, a sign of divine proximity through the presence of the poor. Such dedication was even evident during his final sojourn in Italy where he had gone for respite. Having warmly welcomed local members of the Society of St. Vincent de Paul, he personally attended to the nearby peasants and fishermen. His kindness inspired them to regard him as a saintly visitor. But his weakening condition prompted his family to bring him quickly back to France in 1853. He knew that he was close to the end and wanted to die in the land of his birth. They reached Marseilles on his homeland's southern coast. Solaced by family and friends with comfort and prayers, Frédéric tenderly professed his great love of God[88] and in hushed but distinctive tones prayed for divine mercy before serenely passing away. His funeral in Paris was lovingly and adoringly attended by a throng of colleagues and admirers. With ensuing widespread devotion, prompted by Frédéric's evident sanctity, Pope John Paul II named him blessed in 1997.[89]

BLESSED VICTOIRE RASOAMANARIVO—A MIGHTILY INFLUENTIAL CONVERT

Admired by the nineteenth-century royal court of the land now called Madagascar, cherished by slaves and the downtrodden, revered by the population who shared her faith, the black noblewoman Victoire was a paragon of both modesty and forceful leadership.

As a youth she was influenced by certain non-Christian religious practices. The amulet she wore was believed to safeguard from evil. Her character and early sense of morality were largely due to the influence of her mother, who was widely regarded as a good woman. From her ancestral religion the mom derived universal ethical principles that she taught Victoire to honor, such as the value of honesty, kindness, respect, and gratitude. Victoire's very early years saw the terrible persecution of Christians in her country. But when she was thirteen the then king allowed priests and religious sisters to work openly. Still called simply by the single name Rasoamanarivo, she soon entered the sisters' new school and became ardently interested in Christianity. After a profound spiritual experience in the chapel, she was eventually baptized and assumed a new name, Victoire.

---

88. O'Meara, *Frédéric Ozanam*, 446–47, 454.

89. Slattery, *Blessed Frederic Ozanan*, 3–4, 8, 10–14; Baunard, *His Correspondence*, 403.

Living Fully—Godly Energy

She warmly embraced the church's sacraments and diligently committed to Christian patterns of spirituality and morality.

After her marriage, her husband and an uncle tried for political reasons to lure her from Catholicism. This she strongly and successfully resisted despite her familial attachments. More loyal to the state than to religion, some of her relatives resorted to blatant physical harassment of her, quite ironically at the hands of their slaves—for her distinctively egalitarian disposition toward her own slaves was motivated by her religious sentiment of equality. Every evening they all gathered with her for prayer, not only the household slaves but also those of the surrounding manor. One of her closest friends and confidants was in fact a female slave with whom, as with other friends, she often prayed while daily living the faith without fanfare but with firm commitment.

Though reserved and humble, her spirituality and strength of character were easily discernible but by some cynics not with admiration. Slaves and associates observed her long periods of prayer, day and night. Fortified by such devotions and by frequent worship, her acceptance of responsibilities to her husband and the royal court was enthusiastic, winning her diminished criticism and great respect in official circles. Palatial status scarcely restrained her love of attending to the poor and lepers of her neighborhood by regularly offering them emotional and financial support. Once she even took an impoverished fatherless family into her home for a time.[90] Prisoners, who by the practice of her culture were brutally treated, found encouragement and comfort as she taught them the catechism. She assisted her pastor in his charitable works and substantially provided funding as he oversaw the construction of a cathedral in the capital.

Her husband was no paragon of virtue. Despite his abuse she patiently strove to manifest the love she believed was due him by her marital vows. Such dedication was seen, even by her contemporaries, not as feeble resignation but as steadfastness in the strength of character and religious fervor that marked her from her youth.[91]

During the years when many clergy were forbidden on the island, she would sit contemplatively in church, spiritually content that imaging a Mass would suffice for a time. Chief among her prayerful petitions was one for the return of the missionaries. Frequent among her works was responsible action on behalf of the beleaguered faithful. After three years the

---

90. Fourcadier, *Vie héroïque*, 51, 53.
91. Simon-Perret, *Victoire Rasoamanarivo*, 17–18, 54–55, 59, 70, 75.

missionaries did return, whereupon Victoire retired from her leadership role and resumed her charitable initiatives, especially on behalf of prisoners and lepers. After her husband's death she intensified her prayer life and devoted herself to caring for one of her ailing and destitute uncles, the very one who had been so instrumental in persecuting Christians during the absence of missionaries on the island. Plagued by increasing illness, she could receive the sacraments only at home. Her enthusiastic five-kilometer walk[92] to a procession honoring the Assumption of Mary brought her in 1890 to the brink of death but not to decreased prayer. Victoire passed away as she had lived, in heightened fervor. Upon her death, her face immediately became radiant, transfigured by a discernible smile. At her funeral, an enormous throng grieved with uncommon affection. She was beatified by Pope John Paul II in 1989.[93]

SAINTS LOUIS AND MARIE-AZÉLIE MARTIN— SPIRITUALLY MINDED PARENTS

They were successful nineteenth-century business partners who achieved renown not only for their fine products but, among their dearest associates, for the way in which they managed their household. The family spirit that they nurtured and that endured even after the mother passed away drew admiration well beyond the boundaries of their native France.

Louis and Zélie were a middle-class couple who from the beginning of their marriage in the city of Alençon hoped more in providence than in their acquired wealth. Indeed their spiritual interests meant more to them than the material and social status that they enjoyed. Zélie was extremely cautious of the arrogance and even irreligiousness to which she could succumb because of prosperity. To her the sizableness of wealth should thus not in every case be resented by the less fortunate. Her disposition in this regard was that of a highly ethical woman of tempered material interests who herself produced and marketed luxury items. She was serving many who likely prospered more than she and Louis did, and she was grateful for their business. Louis, who had happily relied on his skills to mount and market exquisite costly diamonds, was likewise so disposed. The couple appreciated finery but was keenly set on the spiritual. They regarded their

---

92. Unienville, "Victoire Rasoamanarivo," paras. 22–24.
93. Marie, "August 8, 2008," para. 20.

Living Fully—Godly Energy

marriage and their business as responses to a divine calling and their children as gifts from heaven.

In such a setting Zélie did not coast blithely without challenges. She found it imperative to control her temper, a force against which she confessed she had to struggle regularly. Her inner strife was exacerbated by the anxiety and depression to which she was prone, undoubtedly incited by the recurrent pain of losing four children in death and of experiencing the proximity of death in the remaining five girls when they were young and sickly. Yet she knew comfort.

Not only by the attention they showed one another but also by the words of their letters, Louis and Zélie demonstrated their deep and devoted mutual love. It was an affection of profound friendship and spiritual bonding. Zélie cherished her closeness to Louis and felt that she could not live without him. He in turn loved her with all his heart, as one dedicated to her for life. When Louis sold his successful and enjoyable watchmaking and jewelry business, his primary motive was to alleviate Zélie's stress in managing her tremendously successful lace enterprise and to have more time for his family. Out of generosity toward them, he gave up his talent and enthusiasm for his accustomed style of artistry.[94]

Their children learned from them how to be generous and how to pray. The couple gently admonished that the girls' devotion and acceptance of daily trials, large and small, should evidence ongoing trust in God. Zélie, who was a member of the Franciscan Third Order, told them stories about favorite saints. Louis was an ardent aficionado of nature, which was to him a striking manifestation of providence. Spending many hours outdoors with his young daughter, Thérèse, he inspired in her an enchantment with the riches of the landscapes and the radiance of the day and night skies. His sensitive disposition also modeled total abandonment to the divine will. Such parental influence would flower in her adult religious life as she with the passing years became revered as St. Therese of Lisieux.

The Martins as a family enjoyed billiards, hiking, fishing, and travel. Louis savored gardening and other forms of relaxation. Yet his enchantment with the outdoors and his penchant for travel were always complemented by his attraction to reverent solitude. He fasted modestly and set aside days in a monastery for religious retreats. In the attic of the family's home in Lisieux he maintained a quiet room for reading, prayer, and meditation. He would invite his daughters to join him there to discuss spiritual matters

---

94. Renda, introduction to *Deeper Love*, xxiv–xxv.

Good and Wealthy

and to grow in appreciation of moral and spiritual values. Attention to spirituality marked the Martins' entire family life. There was more joy than solemnity. The couple attended daily Mass, carefully reserved Sunday as a day of rest and spiritual renewal. They prayed with their children regularly. The family also generously served the poor, sometimes around their own hearth. They brought Zélie's widowered aging father into their home and cared for him until he died.

Louis attended to the poor as a volunteer in the Society of St. Vincent de Paul both in Alençon and Lisieux, something that the Martin girls observed with great admiration.[95] He and Zélie assisted the needy and sick with alms and by support for hospitalization, always discreetly avoiding any fanfare, only with enough visibility to model such action for their children. Generous to the church and its endeavors, the couple regularly donated large sums to a general missionary fund and specifically helped with the expansion of a Canadian seminary. They taught their children to be likewise mission minded.[96]

At the age of forty-five Zélie learned that she had incurable breast cancer. Louis was devastated, numbed to the point of inaction. Though her enthusiasm for the business was waning, Zélie persisted to the end in dedication to her family and the couple's enterprise.[97] For several months she bore the disease with great patience, courage, and faith, ever attempting to console the family rather than seek their consolation. She wanted them to not unduly mourn but to trust in God regarding her destiny and their future family life. Her hopeful trip to Lourdes and its healing waters brought change to her heart but not her body. Despite great pain in her final days, she remained faithfully resigned to her heavenly future.[98]

Having succumbed to the disease rather quickly, her desires for her family would be realized. After her death in 1877, and after the move to Lisieux, the lives of Louis and his daughters continued to breathe of the long-established reverential spirit of the Martin household. The dedicated and loving father oversaw the training, education, and spiritual formation of his daughters, who honored him with devotion and warmest esteem. In the family tradition their days included ample time for regular prayer

---

95. Louis Wust and Marjorie Wust, *Louis Martin*, 78, 80–81, 105, 195.
96. Office of the Postulator General of the Discalced Carmelites, "Profile."
97. Cadéot, *Zélie Martin*, 36, 187.
98. Louis Martin and Zelie Martin, *Deeper Love*, 101, 113, 135, 142, 145, 263, 344–46.

together.[99] In 1894 Louis passed away in Lisieux, seventeen years after Zélie's death, never having remarried. For the greatest part of his life he had enjoyed excellent health and invigorating stamina. But debilitating strokes, which he accepted humbly and graciously, suddenly necessitated extensive hospitalization. Upon his release, he spend the last two years of his life, mostly lucid,[100] in the tender care of two of his daughters. Hopeful of heaven, he passed away peacefully.[101] In 2015 Pope Francis solemnly proclaimed Louis and Zélie saints.[102] Their canonization was the first time in history that a married couple would, at the same time, be so named.[103]

ST. GIANNA BERETTA MOLLA—A PHYSICIAN IN SPIRITUAL RESIDENCY

It was Italy in the 1920s. Guided by her parents, the young Gianna learned at home to appreciate daily worship, regular prayer, and unceasing concern for the poor.[104] Evening recitation of the rosary, with her father leading additional prayers, was an enshrined Beretta family practice. She would pray the rosary daily for the rest of her life, and with her husband after their marriage.[105] A particularly impressive high school retreat enhanced her spiritual sensitivity and attention to community service. Having acquired a healthy appreciation of chastity, she became a role model for her peers. Inspired by her brother's medical service in Brazil, she originally considered becoming a medical missionary. Her university degrees and clinical training would have equipped her eminently for such a vocation. But with a firm commitment to discerning God's will, she realized with the help of a spiritual advisor that she was called to marriage and family life.

Early in her career she made a trip to the shrine in Lourdes, France. Her intent was to provide medical support for pilgrims and to prayerfully seek divine guidance in finding a husband. Pietro, the love of her life, appeared shortly thereafter. For both of them the prospect of marriage was the beginning of a spiritual journey. They regarded their love as divinely

---

99. Di Nicola and Danese, *Amore scritto in cielo*, 86–87, 111–13, 162–63.
100. Piat, *Story of a Family*, 48, 67, 142–59, 171, 176–79, 272, 336, 381–82, 396.
101. Cadéot, *Louis Martin*, 120, 149.
102. Wikipedia, "Louis Martin and Marie-Azélie Guérin," para. 16.
103. Ziegler, "History Awaits," para. 1.
104. Vatican News, "Gianna Beretta Molla (1922–1962)," paras. 1–2.
105. Molla and Guerriero, *Saint Gianna Molla*, 36–37, 61.

induced and sustained. They wanted to dedicate themselves entirely to one another and to have children as a means of cooperating with God's creative plan for humanity. They married in 1955. The ensuing years brightened with the births of their children, and the couple treasured them with hearts of thanks to God. The Molla household was marked by regular family devotion. Every day, except on the hectic mornings when readying the growing and hungry children for nursery school, Gianna attended Mass, as she had since her First Communion at the age of five. Hers was a deep but quiet faith, not one for public display. She was a devoted wife and mother, yet she also voluntarily offered medical help in institutions assisting children and parents of other families.

During times of separation, mostly because of Pietro's business trips, the happy couple wrote to one another frequently, from early in their engagement through the later years of their marriage. Gianna always missed her husband terribly and worried about his safety. The letters are of utmost tenderness and express their warm affection for one another. Clearly they regarded their relationship as a spiritual bond. Their dedication to one another was, along with their joy in one another's presence, quite remarkable amid the ever fluctuating circumstances of their lives. References to such things as air travel and television—striking amid biographies of saints—are reminders that the couple was very much a part of a modern technological era.[106]

They exuberantly enjoyed the world's good things. Pietro once recalled to Gianna how she admirably enjoyed snowy peaks, varied travels, musical performances, live drama, and a gamut of festivities. This made clear to him, he continued, that surrender to the divine will can be saintly without forsaking life's finest pleasures. For him she exemplified that such enjoyment, when temperately combined with devotion to family and dispositions of charity, demonstrates remarkable sensitivity to heavenly grace.

After three problematic and painful yet delightfully successful pregnancies,[107] Gianna's pregnancy of 1961 became complicated by a tumor. She and Pietro faced a dreadful decision, whether she or the infant in her womb should survive if it came to a choice. Catholic teaching would have permitted a hysterectomy, which would be life-saving for her but tragic for the child, who would have died as an unintended effect.[108] Convinced

---

106. Beretta and Molla, *Journey of Our Love*, 45, 148, 193, 275–77.
107. Da Riese Pio X, *Love of Life*, 36–37, 46–47, 54, 128–29, 134–35, 139, 155–56.
108. Heinlein, "St. Gianna Beretta Molla," para. 8.

nonetheless that it would be wrong to let the child die, the couple sadly faced a possible new future: Pietro and the four children might live the remainder of their days without Gianna's loving attention. Though with regret, he accepted Gianna's self-sacrificing disposition and honored her conviction that her call to motherhood would be fulfilled with the birth of what would likely be her final child. Several months later, after the successful delivery of that healthy baby through caesarean section, Gianna succumbed to a terrible, ever-spreading infection. Gianna was able for a time to tenderly gaze into the eyes of the newly arrived little girl but with a saddening prescience of loss.[109] The painful prospect that four children entrusted to their widowed father would grow up without their mother was however transfigured by her utter trust in divine loving providence.

Despite great pain, which she accepted devotedly, she remained strong in her faith and prayerfully sought heavenly comfort and support, professing her love for her Lord and seeking divine help for a holy death. Some have debated the wisdom of Gianna's decision to have the fourth child, but Pietro fully concurred with her commitment and faith. She was soon comatose. In accord with her wishes, Pietro arranged during the Easter week of 1962 to have her brought home. Gianna—the courageous wife, mother, and doctor—had been encouraged by hope for a heavenly future. She finally passed away at thirty-nine years of age. Pietro would be helped by his mother, his sisters, and Gianna's sisters to care for the four children.[110] In 2004, for her life of heightened spirituality, devoted service to others, and the heroic self-sacrifice on behalf of her fourth and last child,[111] Pope John Paul II named Gianna a saint.[112] She was the first married woman to be so proclaimed in the previous one thousand years.[113]

BLESSEDS LUIGI AND MARIA BELTRAME QUATTROCCHI— PROFOUND AND UNCOMMONLY FRUITFUL FAITH

One might wonder how a twentieth-century Italian couple like the Beltrame Quattrocchis could have time for rewarding interior lives when their commitments to one another, their family, their community, and nation

---

109. Brown, *No Greater Love*, 27.
110. Wallace and Jablonski, *Saint Gianna*, 79–80, 88.
111. Pelucchi, *Saint Gianna*, 20, 107, 145.
112. Pastoral Centre, "Life of St. Gianna Beretta Molla," para. 69.
113. Allegri, *Due madri*, 16, 40, 48.

were so pronounced. One might further wonder how such worldly concerns left room for attention to the spiritual. Yet self-possession and spirituality were hallmarks of their lives. As children neither Luigi nor Maria experienced family life in which religious practice was particularly intense. It was a time of widespread anticlericalism and atheism. Yet the influence of elders, particularly the women, in each of these youngster's families kept alive the religious heritage and fostered the children's formal participation in standard religious devotions and practices. Moreover, Luigi's adoptive parents had helped him to learn responsibility and behave according to a noble ethic.

Shortly before his formal courtship with Maria, she awakened in him spiritual hope when he suffered a life-threatening illness. Through a heartfelt missive she had assured him of her prayers and urged him to pray as well, straightaway and always thereafter. All his life he kept in his wallet the religious token enclosed in her letter,[114] but his faith did not significantly grow until after his marriage to her. Spiritual progress for both of them was gradual. By dispositions during their early years together they inclined more to mutual devotion than to God. It was only over time that their heartfelt interest in one another and their children attained its unique fullness, a transforming sense of divine transcendence suffusing their earthly lives. This progress in faith was largely facilitated by conversations with each other, dialogues in which they shared not just the day's events but also their inner experiences, including their spiritual sentiments.

Such communication further profoundly and positively affected their close relationships with their children. It was prayer and her acceptance of the divine will that nurtured Maria's heartfelt welcome of the couple's second child, a little girl whose presence dispelled her motherly doubts about caring for an additional little one just eighteen months after the birth of the first. When confronted with the perceived certainty of Maria's death through the pregnancy of their second daughter and fourth child, the couple's firm rejection of an abortion was immeasurably supported by religious confidence. Their solidarity in the decision was firm, having grown from their gaze upon the cross and the image of the Virgin Mary, who had born Jesus.

The couple's deep love was clearly visible, and they strove to make it so to one another. Luigi was extremely attentive to Maria and treated her with great tenderness. Throughout their nearly fifty years of marriage,

---

114. Vanzan, "Maria e Luigi Beltrame Quattrocchi," 248.

Living Fully—Godly Energy

Maria almost giddily awaited his return home each evening. They showed one another respect, deferred to one another, and sought a harmony nurtured by faith in a supportive God. The couple's bond was thus remarkable. When Maria sometimes referred to Luigi warmly as "Master," or when he on occasion lovingly calls her "Little Madonna," they evidenced mutual respect, each showing a tranquil deference that they believed was divinely sustained. Such reciprocity far transcended the kinds of dominance and subservience typical of many marriages of the time.

All of this hardly left them immune from friction, or from faults they felt free to dutifully call to one another's attention through thoughtful discussion. Maria could be stubbornly set in her ways. Luigi could be unrelentingly impatient. Despite his effort at quitting, Luigi's continued smoking brought to the house a haze that Maria never liked. When such lapses of contentment threatened familial serenity, they discussed the issues in the absence of their children and always turned to one another with forgiveness.

Everyone in the family was a Third Order Franciscan. As a member of this lay spiritual association, Maria exhibited devotional comportment that for a time appeared to Luigi as a displacement of his role in her life. Though she never relinquished a sincere and admirable desire for heightened virtue, she was able to convince him that his discouragement was needless, that her aspirations were in no way distinct from his own goal of heartfelt attentiveness to the divine Spirit. Luigi aspired to deeper intimacy with God, to ever-truer humble conformity with the heavenly will known through wordless communication or starkly silent contemplation. They both made regular spiritual retreats, and Maria enjoyed counseling from prominent priests.

From early on such formative influence spiritually enriched the entire Beltrame Quattrocchi family. A refined sensitivity to providence constrained Maria and Luigi to embrace with enthusiasm the forms of life to which they had been called. Here intimacy with God, they realized, was inextricably linked to intimacy with one another and their offspring. This realization became an ongoing awareness that enhanced not just their closeness to one another but also their profound sensitivity to their children, facilitating bonds that endured even after the young ones became adults and left home.[115]

---

115. Catapano and Angrisani, *Mistica coniugale*, 25–27, 31–40, 97.

Like several other lay women and men in this book, in their younger years Maria and Luigi found the serenity of monastic life alluring. Their call however, they came to heartily believe, was not to live for themselves alone or simply by self-serving wishes. Thus the Beltrame Quattrocchi couple's primary commitment was to their family. Luigi's absence from daily meals was a rarity, solidifying his devotion to his children and Maria. The couple partook diligently in the social, moral, and religious upbringing of their children. In a manner unusual for husbands of his times, Luigi shared with Maria the daily (and nightly!) care and comforting of the young ones.[116] In their later years Luigi's attention was more to their studies and recreation, and Maria's, more to their spiritual formation. Family life was centered on prayer. Luigi frequently prayed at church and daily led the family—along with the household staff—in praying the rosary. This and other family devotions—monthly or annual—occurred in the dining room where a painting of Jesus was conspicuous.

Both Luigi and Maria attended daily Mass, and inspired their children to do the same. Luigi often functioned as a server at the altar. Admirably exemplifying recommendations in Maria's writings, she and Luigi accompanied the children to worship, encouraged their reading spiritual works, engaged them in casual conversation about life, exhorted them to heed respected counsel, and reminded them of the importance of engaging in charitable activities. Religious retreats were also part of the family routines.

Their vacation home in the country contained a small chapel that invited regular devotion in a setting designed for sacramental devotion. Vacationing with the children was for Maria and Luigi not just a time of respite and recuperation but more profoundly a time for spiritual refreshment. Exhilarating hikes and bike rides brought them and the children enjoyment of the divine presence in nature and provided enchantment with singing birds, blazing sunsets, imposing mountains, and burbling waters.

When their two adolescent sons chose to begin their preparations for the priesthood—which they eventually attained—the devoted parents blessed and encouraged them despite initial reservations regarding the boys' academic futures and with resignation to intense parental pangs of separation from their nested young ones. Later, in like circumstances, one of their two daughters became a nun. Maria was deeply grateful for these three initiatives, regarding them as honors and as part of a providential design, while she cherished the nobility of her own vocation to marriage

116. Pasquale, *Luigi e Maria*, 10–11.

Living Fully—Godly Energy

and family. Her devotion to her children extended well beyond their youth. Numerous lengthy letters to the three assigned to religious institutions evidence her continued maternal encouragement and support. Luigi preferred direct interaction. For many years he visited the three on successive weekends every month, departing by train on Saturday in order to be back in the office on Monday.

The couple's famous hospitality was complemented by their gracious response to requests at their home for food, emotional support, or, as we have seen, refuge during World War II.[117] As a couple Maria and Luigi opened their door frequently and generously, not only to entertain, but to provide consolation and encouragement to many struggling with their faith or with various moral challenges. At other times their much sought attention was directed by each of them individually. With her profound spiritual sensitivity, Maria provided counsel to the stream of family members, friends, priests, and nuns who confidently sought her perspectives. With boundless generosity Luigi personally responded to numerous appeals for monetary assistance, whether these came from relatives or strangers, lay persons or clerics, individuals or groups, however near or distant. He was extremely sensitive to others' pain, warmly seeking precise ways to help them.[118] If money was not the issue, Luigi gave welcome counsel and emotional support. And to this he added assistance for many in need of legal representation.

Their religiousness extended, though far more discreetly, into their public lives. With Maria's support Luigi complemented his professional life with charitable and humanitarian activity.[119] Devoting extensive leisure time to youth formation, especially with the Boy Scouts, he was variously honored with awards, none of which he ever referenced to elicit further acclaim. He was simply a focused and avid doer. Luigi professed that a Christian could, even should, strive to acquire riches for himself, his family, and members of society. Yet such aspirations, he believed, had to be subordinate to spiritual goals by which human enterprise became transfused with the divine. Accomplishments like these can only be realized through intentionality guided by religious faith. Should the acquisition of wealth impede personal and social spiritual enrichment, he claimed boldly, it was better to be poor! To be properly focused, he felt, those blessed materially

---

117. O'Neel, *Thirty-Nine New Saints*, 132–33.
118. Maria Beltrame Quattrocchi, *Ordito e la trama*, 5, 10.
119. Dell'Orto, *Sant'insieme*, 2.1.3; 2.2.2.

should heed the counsel of those who have avowedly and devotedly chosen poverty for religious reasons so as to profit from heavenly riches.

Feeling called to enjoy material goods of this world while subordinating them to spiritual and beneficent goals, Luigi enjoyed Maria's full concurrence. In their respective ways—she, through inspiriting publications and generous social service, he, through productive legal services in the political realm, and both, through intense commitment to marriage and family—the couple's lives were extraordinarily rich and enriching.[120] Maria gave of herself in more than academic or professional ways. She served for years in a national program that provided various forms of family assistance,[121] participated in numerous other charitable endeavors, taught catechism classes, helped wounded earthquake victims, provided solace for soldiers during World War I,[122] served voluntarily as a nurse during World War II, and supported the founding of a Catholic university.

Secularists, and even some moral renegades, found uplifting Luigi's obvious but quite reserved religiousness. He professed his faith, but was driven more to express it in deeds. That approach in one instance led to a Freemason's religious conversion. By his fine constitution Luigi overcame three heart attacks in his later years. But the challenges of the times weighed heavily on him: the stresses of World War II, with Italy's occupation by the Nazis, and above all the horrendous plight of Jews to whom he and Maria gave so much assistance.

In 1951 Maria and the seventy-one-year old Luigi delighted in a rare opportunity to gather with all four of their adult children for a Mass in Rome. Four days later he died of a fourth heart attack, having displayed an ardent hope that the faith that so enlivened him would see him through death happily. For many mourners it was the passing of a saint.[123]

In Maria's heart of hearts he was not utterly gone. After forty-six years of abundantly contented marriage, she continued to feel his loving presence, especially through devotions and worship. Increasingly given to prayer, she spent her final years additionally engaged in writing and domestic activity. She lived to be eighty-one. In 1965 the family's summer home was providing her solace, fond memories, and joy. With her was the daughter who had

---

120. Papàsogli, *Quesi borghesi*, 144–49, 155, 179, 182, 190, 210–12, 214–18.

121. Beltrame Quattrocchi, *Ordito e la trama*, 33.

122. Vatican News, "Luigi Beltrame Quattrocchi," para. 19.

123. Beltrame Quattrocchi, *Lui, lei, noi, loro*, 17, 19, 27, 38, 40, 50–52, 60, 74, 85–86, 91–92, 124.

long lived with and ardently served the Beltrame Quattrocchi family, the daughter who many years ago had been rescued from an abortive death by Maria and Luigi's decision to bear her to term. After the call of the nearby church bells, Maria finished her noonday prayer. As she returned from the sunlit garden, her aging heart surrendered. Steadied in the loving arms of that youngest daughter, she stepped toward the household's welcoming shade and passed away.[124] Maria and Luigi were beatified in 2001 by Pope John Paul II,[125] the first time in history that a married couple had been so designated.[126]

---

124. Savior.org, "Blessed Luigi Beltrame Quattrocchi," para. 11; Papàsogli, *Quesi Borghesi*, 336–37.

125. Marie, "April 8, 2008," para. 1.

126. Abbate, *Gesù é il mio unico*, 154.

Conclusion: Illustrious Prosperity— Exemplary Richness

THE TREACHEROUS ALLURE OF WEALTH

ANCIENT ISRAEL SADLY GREW to experience too many of the wealthy who oppressed or exploited the poor (Isa 10:1–2). Jesus remarked that wealth can allure to the point of distracting from what is ultimately more valuable (Matt 13:22). Riches, he also taught, can choke off one's ability to advance in virtue or spirituality (Luke 8:4). Similarly Saint Paul observed that riches can breed noxious appetites that menace daily life and religious faith (1 Tim 6:9–10), as was sadly evident even among some early Christians' deceit, overindulgence, and destructiveness (Jas 5:4–6).

WEALTH AS TREACHEROUS BUT SURMOUNTABLE

The notorious moral indifference and clearly exploitive perniciousness of numerous wealthy elite provided considerable background for Jesus' observations regarding the onerousness if not odiousness of riches. It has been cogently argued that his denigration of wealth is not a sweeping denunciation of abundant ownership but is almost always an indictment of those whose fortunes were derived through unscrupulous treatment of others, especially the poor. The geographical setting, literary context, and precise vocabulary of such censure disclose a mostly Judean—rather than Galilean—environment where abusive taxation, crass monetary dealings, fraud, forceful unjust extraction of income, and corrupt juridical rulings were widespread. Jesus' contemporary audience, whether on hearing him directly or relying on the Gospel accounts, could have thus grasped the

Conclusion: Illustrious Prosperity—Exemplary Richness

implications of the "woes" that Jesus directed against an elite population that dishonored established ethics or Israel's traditional exhortations regarding honest and accommodating commercial dealings.[1] Such elites resemble the first-century rich that James rebukes in his epistle (Jas 5:1–6).

It should be noted that Jesus' wording entails rhetoric of an early Middle-Eastern sort. "Indeed, it is easier for a camel to go through the eye of a needle than for someone who is rich to enter the kingdom of God" (Luke 18:25). Here the rich person's plight should at least be understood as it likely would have commonly been in the Aramaic language of Jesus' culture, or as hyperbole in other cultures or ages. The statement contains a substantial truth made poignant by exaggeration—namely, highlighted as important though not necessarily absolute.[2] In a later Western world one speaking or writing of such a matter might be careful to distinctly characterize the plight of, say, the person unduly attached to things of the world, rather than assert, or at least suggest, that this applies to all who are rich.

Clement of Alexandria (AD 150–215), a prominent theologian of early Christianity, notes that the difficulty associated with a rich person reaching heaven (Mark 10:23; Matt 19:23; Luke 18:24) should not be taken as an impossibility. One could, he says, insolently write off the rich regarding eternal life with God. But such would be a failure to recognize that here Jesus is challenging them to use their wealth in accord with God's designs. Here it is the proper use of wealth that ultimately counts, not necessarily its renunciation. Clement's perspective is corroborated by observations that from the earliest times in the church, there was no general norm for such self-denial, only a recognition of the danger of wealth and its mismanagement.[3] Clement discerned that renunciation of wealth was not an absolute norm and that abundant possession should be combined with compassion for those in need.[4]

The early Middle East—and the larger Greek-speaking world of the gospels—also harkened to Jesus' personalized rhetoric such as, "If you have faith the size of a mustard seed, you will say to this mountain, 'Move from here to there,' and it will move; and nothing will be impossible for you" (Matt 17:20). Clearly the teaching asserts the great power of faith, without suggesting that every hearer could literally move a mountain in this way.

1. Bowyer, *Maker Versus the Takers*, 10–11, 54, 58, 65–66, 72, 113, 139.
2. Hays, *Renouncing Everything*, 32, 73.
3. Hoek, "Widening the Eye," 70–75.
4. McGuckin, "Vine and the Elm," 11–13.

Yet faith of this kind, say the gospels in their characteristic ways, can even give a mere mortal like the apostle Peter the extraordinary ability to walk on water, which he did at least for a time (Matt 12:29). The key to such remarkable capacities is unflinching persistence in faith (Matt 12:31). As we have seen, the saintly personalities we are speaking of here exhibited such faith by disposition, words, and deeds. They exhibited extraordinary faith, virtuous capacities, and exemplary achievements that for countless others remain extreme if not impossible hurdles.

WEALTH AS A BLESSING

Although Solomon as a young king prayed above all for a keen knowledge of right and wrong so that he could duly govern ancient Israel, in a dream God promised him, besides such discernment, incomparable riches and a long life (1 Kgs 3:7–15). Solomon exemplifies the Psalmist's acclamation that guidance from the Lord is more precious than a storehouse of silver and gold (Ps 119:72). But the good king also exemplifies a recipient of wealth divinely granted as a reward for devotion (Prov 10:22). The milk and honey promised by God to a faithful Israel (Exod 3:8) are signs of divinely ordered abundance and prosperity (Ezek 13:13). Jesus observes material abundance as a reward for viewing worldly enjoyments as secondary to religious commitment (Matt 19:29).

A major biographer of Saint Margaret of Scotland, one who knew her personally, was Turgot, the bishop of the Scottish diocese of St. Andrews. Though quite aware of gospel teachings regarding the risk of riches for one's spiritual life, he opined theologically that God lavishly added to Margaret's possessions because of her primary concern for promoting divine interests and the earthly justice associated with them.[5]

Saint Louis made use of money and possessions but was not used by them. He was taken with them, not as ends in themselves but for their ability to open to him a larger dimension where he could see and find his God and God's designs for the world. In Louis' case the locale was the kingdom of France. His hope was for the blessed destiny that he envisioned for France and the distant domains for which he crusaded. He, like Margaret and many other heroes of this book, enjoyed wealth in a way advised through the ages by a host of spiritual writers. What they counseled with regard to

---

5. Turgot, *Dunfermline Vita*, 178.

Conclusion: Illustrious Prosperity—Exemplary Richness

possessions and even one's tenacious strategies was a spirit of detachment, of accepting one's fortune in accord with divine providence.

THE AMBIGUITY OF RICHES

For personalities such as those of this book, material objects and situations—that might otherwise distract from a sense of the holy—serve, one might say, as sacramentals. Rather than persisting as unedifying allurements, the finer things of the world disclose, almost poetically, the higher order of the divine. Richness betokens God's bountiful generosity and serves as an endowment ordered to inspired magnanimity and beneficence. "The sun looks down on everything with its light, and the work of the Lord is full of his glory" (Sir 42:16). The earthly pleasures of these saints are in no need of purgation or elimination. Such appreciation of worldly things and circumstances needs only to be steadfast in devoted attention to that behind them, the world's Creator. Saints like these, not unduly attached to riches, typically but inconsequentially recognized their attraction to vowed poverty or to the contemplative or monastic life. Such an attraction highlights saintly success in seeing beyond and surmounting undue worldly attachments. The saintly Margaret, Louis, Elzéar, Delphine, Frédéric Ozanam, Louis Martin, and the Beltrame Quattrocchi couple recognized the attraction but responded with loving diligence to thrive spiritually amid their prosperity.

One may reasonably wonder why such devoted people did not in fact choose to become like the vast majority of other saintly faithful who were poor by lot or choice, the myriad others who found in poverty a root of holiness. In answer to this query it may reasonably be surmised that they found themselves among the notable minority for whom the attainment or retention of wealth could, in response to what they believed was a divine call to faith and charity, be responsibly enjoyed. And enjoy them they did. Yet their riches were a pittance to them, a pittance compared with the wealth of the realm they enjoyed by faith. Within the confines of abundance, plentitude by which they enriched the lives of others, they inhabited a domain fortifying them with grace, friendship, and love, a heavenly realm replete with joy and glory.

Wealth can indeed lead to selfishness and exploitation, frightful banes for the poor. When wealth succumbs to such vices, it is not the major problem. But greed or acquisitiveness is. None of the prosperous venerables, blesseds, and saints treated in this book ultimately fell victims to either. They were saved from such flaws through the graces of compassion and generosity. Saint Louis was especially careful to deter greed and exploitation in his kingdom's feudal economy. Justice on the social scale and generosity on the individual scale especially serve as an antidote to the wealthy individual's potential for greed, a vice fueled by egoism, or for acquisitiveness with its undue attention to material things. Frédéric Ozanam noted that charity is the rival of egoism.[6] Wealth yields in the lives of the saintly neither to acquisitiveness nor to greed's poison but to generosity that nurtures the greatest joys. Jesus conjoins caution about wealth with the observation that with God's help it is indeed possible for the rich to attain salvation (Mark 10: 27; Matt 19:26; Luke 18:27). He thus affirms words of ancient Israel professing that wealth enjoyed in a sinless way is indeed a good thing (Sir 13:24).

So the saintly lives being recounted here in no manner exemplify fidelity to a "prosperity gospel." Such a profession would be adherence to a teaching understood—and perhaps at times caricatured—as a guarantee of, and right to, wealth for the true believer.[7] A "gospel" of this sort would have been foreign to them—as would motivation wherein prosperity is construed, in an essentially philosophical manner, as integrally ensconced in a holistic and wholesome pursuit of abundance.[8] The primary inspiration of our heroes was not attainment of prosperity but the accomplishment of spiritual ends—a goal they would have called doing God's will and thus living "abundantly" (John 10:10)—through faith and charity. Clearly all of them, such as the Beltrame Quattrocchi couple, could be grateful for their wealth as a blessing but in no way be guided by a material profit motive to live in a saintly way.

RICHES AND RESPONSIBILITY

Such disposition toward wealth accords with the Bible's recurrent concern—throughout its two testaments—for the poor; they are beloved of God, and believers or the spiritually minded should dutifully care for them.[9] Both Israel (e.g., Ps 112) and Christianity (e.g., 2 Cor 9) could regard

6. Sickinger, *Antoine Frédéric Ozanam*, 154.
7. Spadaro, "Prosperity Gospel."
8. E.g., Jones, *Art of Abundance*.
9. Lohfink, *Option for the Poor*.

Conclusion: Illustrious Prosperity—Exemplary Richness

riches as a sometime reward for virtue, gifts from God that prove their true worth when shared with those who are impoverished. Even as the God of infinite love imparts life and grace to finite humans who, compared with divine abundance, are deprived or poor, so should believers, like their Lord, render charity toward those in need. A notable characteristic of the wealthy and saintly personalities of this book is their generosity toward the disadvantaged or desolate. Such magnanimity and selflessness well constitute their attention to and love of the poor. Frédéric Ozanam eloquently exhorted his followers, "It is for you, dear brothers, to place yourselves between the rich and the poor, in the name of Jesus Christ, the God of the poor and of the rich, the greatest of the rich since He is rich by nature, and the most holy of the poor since He is poor by the free choice of His love."[10] Using earthly riches to serve the impoverished is a means of allowing prosperity's abundance to mingle in a heavenly way with the precious needs of those who are not only impoverished but also divinely cherished. According to Ozanam, charity was a duty not only of his society but of all in the larger community. From this perspective Ozanam stands in manifest solidarity with all the other saintly figures of this book in that they dedicated themselves to relieving the anguish of impoverishment.

This does not mean necessarily that saintly forms of love or charity as here exhibited provide universal norms, strategies, or structures for responsibly attending to the poor, let alone for attempting to eradicate poverty.[11] It has even been argued, though quite debatably, that there are better ways to help the poor than by the kinds of charity that most of the prosperous men and women of this book extended.[12] Such a contention is expounded within the parameters of particular social and economic persuasions. The various methods of charity dear to this book's protagonists were practical measures, respectively, within the then ambient socioeconomic systems, to include in good conscience generous attention to the poor as a feature of religious devotion and civic mindedness. One such as Ozanam exemplified this while looking to the Bible and the ideals of the church for suitable guidance. Saint Guntram's wealth and kingly authority brought him much power and influence. Having abandoned the carefree and notorious comportment of his earlier years, as man of wisdom he learned that the greater welfare of the citizenry lay in a reciprocal relationship between

---

10. Scott, "Frédéric Ozanam," 49.
11. Ward, *Wealth*, 210–32.
12. Theoharis, *Always with Us?*, 145–47.

civil and ecclesiastical governance. The institutions and goals of the monarchy, which frequently overlapped with those of the church, could best be achieved when both monarchy and church worked hand in hand, when both welcomed one another's services. Saint Ferdinand III, refusing to rule autocratically, refined his kingly decrees according to the counsel of officials carefully selected from various sectors of his kingdom. Dialogue and subsidiarity clearly marked his executive initiatives. Saints Margaret of Scotland and Adelaide supported and abetted spiritual renewal, thus helping the church better nurture a responsible citizenry.

Though ultimately a proponent of democracy, Ozanam admired the kingship of Saint Louis, whose reign he revered as self-sacrificing rather than exploitive. Undoubtedly Ozanam would have included Saint Margaret of Scotland in Louis's ranks. For she ruled primarily with her people's good in mind. Sensitivity to them and practical attention to their needs could best be realized, she thought, by an effective governmental structure in close contact with the citizenry but kept as streamlined as possible. In Ozanam's view the ideal monarch should be the servant of the entire nation, not merely of her or his palatial domain. Whether royal or not, the attention to the poor extended by other prosperous saintly persons treated here is likewise deserving of esteem and apposite imitation. Surely such charity provides, even today, inspiration and encouragement in numerous ways for dutiful, helpful, and creative attention to the less fortunate. Ozanam's accord with such a perspective, and even his own lifelong generous expenditures on behalf of the needy[13] do not however gainsay the way in which he stands in stark contrast with the other saints, blesseds, and venerables depicted here—namely, by his dedication to undoing neglect of certain social conditions contributing to the plight of the poor. One may argue to what extent most of the heroes in this book should be faulted for exhibiting charity primarily in the conventional ways of almsgiving and humanitarian service. Considering the heroes' historical circumstances, such an argument would seemingly be tenuous. Admittedly the majority of them did not dedicate themselves as well to what was dear to Ozanam—namely, such charity combined with social reform.

The undisputable fact that in multiple cases wealth or high finance is problematic, discomforting, or even scandalous accords with the opinion of many that it is wrong, or at least a necessary evil. Such a view, fueling the flame of conviction that the pursuit of wealth is inherently exploitative

---

13. Mercier, "Ozanam et la misère," 60.

Conclusion: Illustrious Prosperity—Exemplary Richness

or predatory, equates abuses in the pursuit with the pursuit itself. For a counter opinion one might turn to an elaborate philosophy of self-interest to demonstrate that wealth, productivity, or profit-seeking can be morally acceptable or even praiseworthy.[14] But the terms of such a theoretical rebuttal of the depreciating opinion of financial prosperity could themselves be problematic,[15] say by evoking empathy for inordinate individualism or selfishness. One of America's greatest statesmen, President Theodore Roosevelt (1858–1919), poignantly articulated a balanced view regarding the hazardous potential of both wealth and poverty:

> We of the great modern democracies must strive unceasingly to make our several countries lands in which a poor man who works hard can live comfortably and honestly, and in which a rich man cannot live dishonestly nor in slothful avoidance of duty; and yet we must judge rich man and poor man alike by a standard which rests on conduct and not on caste, and we must frown with the same stern severity on the mean and vicious envy which hates and would plunder a man because he is well off and on the brutal and selfish arrogance which looks down on and exploits the man with whom life has gone hard.[16]

Such are the words of one of America's most beloved presidents, who, long after his governmental accomplishments, sought vociferously a "square deal" for all the citizenry.[17] This was the quite wealthy man who, through service and legislation, diligently and effectually worked to reverse the plight of the countless poor or underprivileged who were oppressed by the ravages of exploitative or cruelly negligent elements of wealthy magnates and their industries. He was a man of great means who in principle distrusted the leadership competencies of "the moneyed classes, especially those of large fortune."[18]

This book can be taken in part as an argument against sweeping disdain for the wealthy or prosperous. The theological polemic here however is not primarily theoretical but historical, turning to the living witness of

---

14. Brook and Watkins, introduction to *In Pursuit of Wealth*, vii–viii; Brook and Watkins, "Turning the Tables," 183–86.

15. Dodson, "Ayn Rand's Philosophy."

16. Roosevelt, *Theodore Roosevelt*, 5.

17. Roosevelt, *Theodore Roosevelt*, 490.

18. Roosevelt to Frederick Scott Oliver, Aug. 9, 1906, quoted in Ruddy, *Roosevelt's History*, 47.

wealthy women and men whose lives have been not only commendable but also saintly. What attention to self is part of such persons' motivation is not constrictive selfishness but the virtuous self-satisfaction that is part of charity—namely, faith-driven love of God, neighbor, and oneself.

If the commitment, drive, and extraordinary achievements of the prosperous personalities of this book can be called inspiring and exemplary, then their exploits may also be called heroic. Viewed this way, the venerable, blessed, and saintly women and men recounted here are heroes indeed. As such heroes and by their prosperity they all enjoyed a state of financial inequality vis-a-vis most of the other citizens of their lands; and they could not, responding rightly to queries about it, deny the fact. Some of them were nobles—like Saint Guntram, Saint Adelaide, and Blessed Victoire Rasoamanarivo—who essentially inherited their wealth. Some of them were entrepreneurs—like Saint Homobonus, Venerable Pierre Toussaint, and Saint Marie-Azélie Martin—who produced wealth or desired possessions for themselves or others. Some of them—like Saint Gianna Molla and the saintly couple Luigi and Maria Beltrame Quattrocchi—served others through beneficence or teaching. Surely by their faith they prized the belief that all persons, created in the divine image, are in essence of equal value and enjoy equal dignity. While not denying the circumstantial inequality that existed among the citizenry of their respective societies, these heroes worked not to eliminate inequality but to reduce it. While their lives suggest the inference that inequality was undeniably part of society's fabric, their deeds model efforts to lessen the ravages of glaring financial disparity. This they all did by their notable attention to helping the poor. Even Frédéric Ozanam, who among our heroes spoke the most vehemently and explicitly of structural needs for poverty's diminishment, implies that financial inequality is an ongoing condition but that it should be significantly reduced; it should not ravage but should be eroded as those who have more move to fairly and effectively better the circumstances of those who have less.

If the prosperous women and men of this book can be faulted for anything, it might be for sometimes fostering or sustaining among the poor an excessive sense of victimhood rather than helping the impoverished to draw in due time on some of their own resources as helps to overcoming their plight, thus avoiding the kind of idleness that Saint Paul regarded as inappropriate (2 Thess 3:10–11). Pope Francis has taught emphatically that financial assistance of the poor should ideally remain temporary. Thus poverty is best eroded by ample varied occasions for productive work through

Conclusion: Illustrious Prosperity—Exemplary Richness

which self-enrichment and a heightened sense of dignity are attained. Social systems, he asserts, can be oriented in this direction—namely, toward a form of practical charity—with the help of appropriate political projects, serviceable education, and humanely sensitive businesses.[19] Ozanam asserted in both his earliest and maturer writings[20] that besides a helping hand, the poor need genuinely friendly assistance in discerning that they can contribute to their world in truly valuable ways. Pierre Toussaint acted on a similar view by training hapless youths for new professions. Empress Adelaide supported those of lesser means until they on their own could turn a profit. One of Ozanam's most heralded achievements was helping a single mother free herself from poverty. Adherents of Ozanam's approach in this regard have come to advocate "systemic change"[21]—namely, supplementing alleviation of present needs with guidance toward personal gain, thereby cooperating with the needy in order to identify and undo the strictures that bind them to poverty.[22] In a democracy or republic both the rich and the poor can and should benefit from initiatives that justly further the interests of both and thus lessen the divide between them. Such cooperation, Ozanam felt, is best achieved by individuals and groups of the populace, especially when motivated by charity; unjust economic inequality cannot be overcome chiefly or exclusively by programs of the government. On the other hand, he thought that diminution of poverty could not be achieved through a totally free or unregulated market.[23]

Proponents of a "prosperity gospel" have been vigorously faulted for a presumptuous view of faith's power to enrich and for lack of compassion for the poor, who by this "gospel" are responsible for their own economic want.[24] But perhaps such heralds of prosperity can at least be affirmed for their sincere attempts to challenge the poor to some creative faith-filled form of self-help. All of this is not to deny that, whatever social or economic challenge there may be, charity best begins, as it did for the saintly philanthropists of this book, with compassion.

---

19. Francis, *Fratelli tutti*, paras. 123, 162, 168, 183, 186–87.
20. Bernardelli, *Storia*, 28.
21. VincentWiki, "Systemic Change," paras. 1–2.
22. Sickinger, *Antoine Frédéric Ozanam*, 126, 153–54, 168, 231–33, 238.
23. Mousin, "Frédéric Ozanam," 66, 76–77.
24. Spadaro, "Prosperity Gospel," paras. 1–2, 4, 24, 27.

Good and Wealthy

ABOVE AND BEYOND

Beyond pecuniary generosity, the heroes of this book abounded in other virtues intrinsic to their spiritual lives. Consistently accompanying material or financial support was their kindly personal service—namely, practical and efficient provision of other kinds of needed attention or assistance. Queen Margaret of Scotland washed the feet of the poor at her door. King Ferdinand helped cook for the impoverished. King Louis once carried stones to help monks build their churches. Professor Frédéric Ozanam had delivered firewood to the desolate. Monsieur Pierre Toussaint taught poor boys income-earning skills. Lady Victoire remained wholeheartedly dedicated to her husband, despite her aversion to his habitual philandering; and her kind endurance led to his conversion. Doctor Gianna Molla brought healing medicine to the indigent sick. Signora Maria Beltrame Quattrocchi comforted those wounded by war. Services such as these typified charity of a refined kind.

The saintly prosperous who wielded authority demonstrated the value of graciousness and consideration for those who served them. Such attention engendered loyalty in these heroes' subjects, attendants, or employees. The mutual respect that was therefore demonstrated by such loyalty facilitated the smooth and profitable operation of the household, enterprise, or region. Saintly virtue animated expeditious oversight.

The lives of these prosperous heroes also exhibited wholesome familial togetherness. A shining feature of their households was the education of children in authentic religious devotion and practice. This had been evidenced as well in the upbringing and education that the saintly themselves had received. The biographer Bishop Turgot obviously admired St. Margaret of Scotland for her having taught her children not just to appreciate prosperity but to strive for it. Behind the author's perspective was his greater appreciation for her teaching them that their immediate goal should be the accomplishment of God's will. With such fervor, she taught, came many rewards, mostly spiritual but including secondarily the benefits of riches. Similarly, Luigi Beltrame Quattrocchi advocated that in heeding the divine will above all one could be inclined to strive in a commendable way for wealth.

This book's heroes did not take their prosperity for granted but abounded in gratitude for it as a blessing in which they could rightly delight. Saint Louis taught his son that such gratitude could result in worthiness to receive a divine gift of more wealth should it be bestowed. Thankfulness of

Conclusion: Illustrious Prosperity—Exemplary Richness

this sort is no consumerist quest for monetary or material rewards above all or for sanctity in order to generate financial gain.

Gratitude for prosperity needed hardly reflect disdain for intentional poverty when seeking to lead a saintly life. Saints such as Margaret, Ferdinand, and Louis affirmed the eminent desirability of elective or vowed poverty by supporting religious communities where forsaking wealth was an essential characteristic of the monastic or communal lifestyle. Louis even encouraged his children to consider aspiring to such poverty. When all of them decided otherwise, he accepted their decisions respectfully and lovingly. Though comfortable in the style of the successful family and civil life which they had attained, the Beltrame Quattrocchis fondly supported three of their children's entry into the priesthood or vowed religious life.

Virtually every saintly personality whose lives and virtues we have surveyed supported institutional religion, in each of their cases Christianity. They financed the construction of imposing churches, cathedrals, and devotional centers. They supported bishops and abbots in an effort to spur spiritual reform where piety lacked fervor, sincerity, or regular private and public practice. The motives of such saintly heroes of this book was not merely personal spiritual enthusiasm or an evangelistic propensity to spread the faith and multiply its adherents. In every case it was their belief as well that widespread religious devotion worked eminently for the good of their domains, for civility and productivity in the societies of which they were part. Religious practice hardly guaranteed the absence of egregious wrongdoing. This the saintly women and men of this book would not deny. Yet their prevailing disposition and practice reflected commitment to organized religion as essentially society's salutary leaven.

The venerable, blessed, and saintly men and women portrayed here are of partly vintage and partly recent historical stock, but all are timelessly relevant. They endure, valuable as role models for the many individuals at pinnacles of great fortunes who publicly reflect today the awesome interplay of wealth and beneficence.[25] But the saintly women and men of this book represent as well the many prosperous women and men who, often unheralded, laudably respond to social need in many ways.[26] This book's heroes did not establish the kingdom of heaven on earth. But their

---

25. Berkman, "Sixteen Jews"; Bukszpan, "Mega-Philanthropists"; Find Some Money, "Catholic Philanthropists"; Inside Philanthropy, "Jewish Foundations"; Jones, "Hush-Hush"; Wikipedia, "List of Philanthropists"; Kumar, "Philanthropist Billionaires"; Martin and Loudenback, "Most Generous."

26. "Who Gives Most to Charity?"

virtuous lives serve as beacons of hope to the prosperous who long for such a divinely founded kingdom. High moral standards can lift one above the ravages that riches can wreak. Generosity can complement the divine grace that this book's heroes believed was the ultimate source of all well-being. Holy women and men like these inspired their contemporaries, provoked edification in ensuing times, and can still enlighten those seeking to enjoy prosperity graciously.

Bibliography

Abbate, Agatina. *Gesù é il mio unico amore: Teresa Di Lisieux, Giorgio La Pira, Luigi E Maria Beltrame Quattrocchi; Tre esperienze di santità, unico cammino per tutti.* Vatican: Lateran University Press, 2009.
African American Registry. "Pierre Toussaint, Businessman and Philanthropist." https://aaregistry.org/story/pierre-toussaint-businessman-and-philanthropist/.
Allegri, Renzo. *Le due madri di papa Wojtyla: Emilia Kaczorowska e Gianna Beretta Molla.* Milan: Ancora, 2012.
Arduino, Fabio. "San Fernando III: Re di Leon e di Castiglia." *Santi, Beati e Testimoni*, last updated May 5, 2007. http://www.santiebeati.it/dettaglio/55200.
Ballan, Mohamad. "The Tomb of Ferdinand III (d. 1252) in Seville: Emblem of Convivencia or Symbol of Reconquista?" *Ballandalus* (blog), Apr. 22, 2015. https://ballandalus.wordpress.com/2015/04/22/7657/.
Bäumer, Gertrud. *Otto I. und Adelheid.* Tübingen: Rainer Wunderlich, 1961.
Baunard, Monsignor. *Ozanam in His Correspondence.* Translated by a Member of the Council of Ireland of the Society of St. Vincent de Paul. New York: Benziger, 1925.
Beltrame Quattrocchi, Maria. *L'ordito e la trama: Radiografia de un matrimonio.* Rome: Fondazione Beltrame Quattrocchi, 2001.
Beltrame Quattrocchi, Tarcisio. *Lui, lei, noi, loro: I beati Luigi e Maria Beltrame Quattrocchi; Testimonianze dirette.* Rome: Cantagalli, 2002.
Bennett, S. A. "Guntramnus, King of Burgundy." In *A Dictionary of Christian Biography and Literature to the End of the Sixth Century A.D., with an Account of the Principal Sects and Heresies*, edited by Henry Wace and William C. Piercy, 432–33. Peabody, MA: Hendrickson, 1999. https://www.ccel.org/ccel/wace/biodict.html?term=Guntramnus,%20king%20of%20Burgundy.
Beretta, Gianna and Pietro Molla. *The Journey of Our Love: The Letters of Saint Gianna Beretta and Pietro Molla*, edited by Elio Guerriero. Translated by Ann Brown. Boston: Pauline, 2014.
Beretz, Elaine M. "Ferdinand III of Castile." In *Holy People of the World: A Cross-Cultural Encyclopedia*, edited by Phyllis G. Jestice, 276. Santa Barbara, CA: ABC-CLIO, 2004.
Berkman, Jacob. "Sixteen Jews Among Chronicle of Philanthropy's Top 50 donors." *Jewish Telegraphic Agency*, Feb. 4, 2009. https://www.jta.org/2009/02/04/united-states/sixteen-jews-among-chronicle-of-philanthropys-top-50-donors.
Bernard, Suzanne. *Les époux vierges: Elzéar de Sabran et Delphine de Signe.* Paris: Perrin, 1994.

Bibliography

Bernardelli, Giorgio. *Storia di F. Ozanam: L'uomo che non aveva paura della crisi.* Turin: Lindau, 2013.

Boillon, Claude. "San Gontranno (Guntramno): Re dei Franchi." *Santi, Beati e Testimoni,* last updated Mar. 2, 2009. http://www.santiebeati.it/dettaglio/47500.

Bonometti, Pietro. "L'iconografia dimezzata: Tentativo per una ricostrizione." In *Omobono: La figura del santo nell'iconografia; Secoli XIII—XIX,* edited by Pietro Bonometti, 23–33. Milan: Silvana editoriale, 1999.

Bowyer, Jerry. *The Maker Versus the Takers: What Jesus Really Said About Social Justice and Economics.* New York: Post Hill, 2020.

Brook, Yaron and Don Watkins. Introduction to *In Pursuit of Wealth: The Moral Case for Finance,* edited by Yaron Brook and Don Watkins, vii–x. Santa Ana, CA: Ayn Rand Institute, 2017.

———. "Turning the Tables on the Inequality Alarmists." In *In Pursuit of Wealth: The Moral Case for Finance,* edited by Yaron Brook and Don Watkins, 173–86. Santa Ana, CA: Ayn Rand Institute, 2017.

Brown, Ann M. *No Greater Love: Bl. Gianna; Physician, Mother, Martyr.* New Hope, KY: New Hope, 1999.

Bukszpan, Daniel. "Meet Today's Mega-Philanthropists: They're Super Rich and Super Generous." *Fortune,* Mar. 19, 2015. https://fortune.com/2015/03/19/philanthropists-billionaires-charity/.

Burke, Raymond L. "Saint Gianna Beretta Molla: Wife, Mother and Physician." Catholic Culture. https://www.catholicculture.org/culture/library/view.cfm?recnum=6234.

Butler, Alban. *Butler's Lives of the Saints,* edited by Herbert J. Thurston and Donald Attwater. 4 vols. Westminster, MD: Christian Classics, 1990. https://archive.org/details/ButlersLivesOfTheSaintsCompleteEdition/mode/2up.

Butler, Alban, and Paul Burns. *Butler's Lives of the Saints.* Concise ed. Collegeville, MN: Liturgical, 2003.

Cadéot, Robert. *Louis Martin: "Père incomparable" de Sainte Thérèse de l'Enfant-Jésu.* Paris: V.A.L., 1985.

———. *Zélie Martin: "Mere incomparable" de Sainte Thérèse de l'Enfant-Jésu.* Paris: V.A.L., 1990.

Campbell, Thomas. "St. Adelaide." In *The Catholic Encyclopedia.* Vol. 1. New York: Robert Appleton, 1907. http://www.newadvent.org/cathen/01140c.htm.

Cantor, Norman F. *The Civilization of the Middle Ages.* New York: Harper, 1994.

Carr, Gregory. "St. Elzéar of Sabran." In *The Catholic Encyclopedia.* Vol. 5. New York: Robert Appleton, 1909. https://www.newadvent.org/cathen/05397a.htm.

Catapano, Erminia and Vincenzo Angrisani. *Mistica coniugale: Luigi e Maria Beltrame Quattrocchi.* Vatican: Libreria Editrice Vaticana, 2006.

Cholvy, Gérard. *Le christianisme a besoin de passeurs.* Perignan, FR: Artège, 2012.

Da Riese Pio X, D. *For the Love of Life: Gianna Beretta Molla, Doctor and Mother.* 2nd ed. N.p.: n.p., 1981.

de Dinechin, Renauld, et al. *Frédéric Ozanam: L'homme d'une promesse.* Paris: Desclée de Brouwer, 2010.

de Joinville, Jean. *The Life of St. Louis.* Translated by René Hague. New York: Sheed & Ward, 1955.

Dell'Orto, Gabriella. *"Sant'insieme": In Dio l'amore é per sempre; Maria e Luigi Beltrame Quattrocchi, storia e testimonianze epistolari di un cammino di santità coniugale.* Scotts Valley, CA: CreateSpace Independent, 2015. Kindle.

BIBLIOGRAPHY

Di Nicola, Giulia Paola and Attilio Danese. *Un amore scritto in cielo: Luigi Martin e Zelia Guérin*. Milan: San Paolo, 2010.

Dodson, Christopher. "Ayn Rand's Philosophy Incompatible with Catholic Teaching." North Dakota Catholic Conference, June 2011. https://ndcatholic.org/yourresources/editorials/column0611/.

Donovan, Stephen. "Blessed Delphine." In *The Catholic Encyclopedia*. Vol. 4. New York: Robert Appleton, 1908. http://www.newadvent.org/cathen/04701a.htm.

Dunlop, Eileen. *Queen Margaret of Scotland*. Edinburgh: NMSE, 2005.

Epple, Dorothea Marie. "Women of Faith: Inspiration for Social Work." *Social Work and Christianity* 39 (Fall 2012) 340–52.

Fernández de Castro Cabeza, Maria del Carmen. *The Life of the Very Noble King of Castile and León, Saint Ferdinand III*. Translated and edited by Foundation for a Christian Civilization. New York: Foundation for a Christian Civilization, 1987.

Find Some Money. "Catholic Philanthropists Who Help People in Need." Last updated Oct. 29, 2015. http://findsomemoney.com/threads/catholic-philanthropists-who-help-people-in-need.583/.

Fitzhenry, James. *Saint Fernando III: A Kingdom for Christ*. St. Marys, KS: Catholic Vitality, 2011.

Folz, Robert. *Les saints roi du Moyen Âge en Occident (VIe–XIIe Siècle)*. Subsidia Hagiographica 76. Brussels: Société des Bollandistes, 1984.

Fourcadier, Etienne. *La vie héroïque de Victoire Rasoamanarivo*. 2nd ed. Paris: Dillen, 1937.

Francis. *Fratelli tutti*. Encyclical letter. Vatican website. Oct. 3, 2020. http://www.vatican.va/content/francesco/en/encyclicals/documents/papa-francesco_20201003_enciclica-fratelli-tutti.html.

Gaposchkin, M. Cecilia. "Boniface VIII, Philip the Fair, and the Sanctity of Louis IX." *Journal of Medieval History* 29.1 (2003) 1–26. doi.org/10.1016/S0304-4181(02)00054-4.

———. "Legende des Hailigen Ellzearius, Die." In *Four Franciscan Saints Lives: German Texts from Codex Sangallensis 589*, edited by Patricia A. Giangrosso, 138–45. Stuttgart: Hanz-Dieter Heinz, Akadmischer Verlag, 1987.

Giangrosso, Patricia A., ed. *Four Franciscan Saints' Lives: German Texts from Codex Sangallensis 589*. Stuttgart: Hanz-Dieter Heinz, Akademischer Verlag, 1989.

———. *The Making of Saint Louis: Kingship, Sanctity, and Crusade in the Later Middle Ages*. Ithaca, NY: Cornell University Press, 2008.

Gilsdorf, Sean. Introduction to *Queenship and Sanctity: The Lives of Mathilda and the Epitaph of Adelheid*, 1–67. Translated by Sean Gilsdorf. Washington, DC: Catholic University of America Press, 2004.

———. Notes to *Queenship and Sanctity: The Lives of Mathilda and the Epitaph of Adelheid*, 186–194. Translated by Sean Gilsdorf. Washington, DC: Catholic University of America Press, 2004.

Golinelli, Paolo. *Adelaide: Regina santa d'Europa*. Milan: Java Book, 2000.

Goullet, Monique. "De Hrotsvita de Gandersheim à Odilon de Cluny: Images d'Adélaïde en l'an mil." In *Adélaïde de Bourgogne: Genèse et représentations d'une sainteté impériale*, edited by Patrick Corget et al., 43–54. Paris: Editions Universitaires de Dijon, 2002.

Goyau, Georges. "St. Louis IX." In *The Catholic Encyclopedia*. Vol. 9. New York: Robert Appleton, 1910. https://www.newadvent.org/cathen/09368a.htm.

Bibliography

Grégoire de Tours. *Histoire des Francs: Livre huitième*, edited by François-Dominique Fournier. In *Collection des mémoires relatifs à l'histoire de France, depuis la fondation de la monarchie française jusqu'au 13 siècle*, edited by François Guizot. Paris: J. L. J. Brière, 1969. http://remacle.org/bloodwolf/historiens/gregoire/francs8.htm.

Gregory of Tours. *History of the Franks: Book IX*, edited by Paul Halsall. Translated by Earnest Brehaut. Fordham University, Internet History Sourcebooks Project. https://sourcebooks.fordham.edu/basis/gregory-hist.asp#book9.

Guerriero, Elio. Introduction to *The Journey of Our Love: The Letters of Saint Gianna Beretta and Pietro Molla*, by Elio Guerriero and Pietro Molla, 1–44, edited by Elio Guerriero. Translated by Ann Brown. Boston: Pauline, 2014.

Hanley, Boniface. "Pierre Toussaint." EWTN. https://www.ewtn.com/catholicism/library/pierre-toussaint-5913.

Harrison, Carol E. *Romantic Catholics: France's Postrevolutionary Generation in Search of a Modern Faith*. Ithaca, NY: Cornell University Press, 2014.

Hays, Christopher M. *Renouncing Everything: Money and Discipleship in Luke*. Mahwah, NJ: Paulist, 2016.

Heckmann, Ferdinand. "St. Ferdinand III." In *The Catholic Encyclopedia*. Vol. 6. New York: Robert Appleton, 1909. https://www.newadvent.org/cathen/06042a.htm.

Heinlein, Michael R. "St. Gianna Beretta Molla: A Saint for the Unborn." Simply Catholic. https://www.simplycatholic.com/st-gianna-beretta-molla/.

Heinzelmann, Martin. *Gregory of Tours: History and Society in the Sixth Century*. Translated by Christopher Carroll. Cambridge: Cambridge Universiy Press, 2001.

Hoek, Annewies van den. "Widening the Eye of the Needle—Wealth and Poverty in the Works of Clement of Alexandria." In *Wealth and Poverty in Early Church and Society*, edited by Susan R. Holman, 67–75. Grand Rapids: Baker Academic, 2008.

Honner, John. *Love and Politics: the Revolutionary Frederic Ozanam*. Melbourne: David Lovell, 2007.

Huddleston, Gilbert. "St. Margaret of Scotland." In *The Catholic Encyclopedia*. Vol. 9. New York: Robert Appleton, 1910. https://www.newadvent.org/cathen/09655c.htm.

Hunter-Blair, Oswald. "Abbey of Dunfermline." In *The Catholic Encyclopedia*. Vol. 5. New York: Robert Appleton, 1909. https://www.newadvent.org/cathen/05192a.htm.

Huntington, Joanna. "St Margaret of Scotland: Conspicuous Consumption, Genealogical Inheritance, and Post-Conquest Authority." *Journal Of Scottish Historical Studies* 33.2 (Nov. 2013) 149–64.

Inside Philanthropy. "Jewish Foundations: Grants for Nonprofits." https://www.insidephilanthropy.com/jewish-funders.

Jones, Arthur. *Pierre Toussaint*. New York: Doubleday, 2003.

Jones, Bob. "Hush-Hush—What Makes Christian Philanthropy Christian?" *World Magazine*, Oct. 26, 1996. https://wng.org/articles/hush-hush-what-makes-christian-philanthropy-christian-1618205584.

Jones, Dennis Merritt. *The Art of Abundance: Ten Rules for a Prosperous Life*. New York: TarcherPerigee, 2018.

Keene, Catherine. *Saint Margaret, Queen of the Scots: A Life in Perspective*. New York: Palgrave Macmillan, 2013.

Kitchen, John. *Saints' Lives and the Rhetoric of Gender: Male and Female in Merovingian Hagiography*. New York: Oxford University Press, 1998.

Bibliography

Kumar, Anugrah. "Over 125 Philanthropist Billionaires Are Giving Half of Their Wealth Away." *The Christian Post*, July 21, 2014. https://www.christianpost.com/news/over-125-philanthropist-billionaires-are-giving-half-of-their-wealth-away.html.

Laurentie, Joseph. *Saint Ferdinand*. 2nd ed. Paris: Victor Legoffre, 1910.

Lee, Hannah Farnham Sawyer. *Memoir of Pierre Toussaint: Born a Slave in St. Domingo*. Westport, CT: Negro Universities Press, 1970.

Le Goff, Jacques. *Saint Louis*. Translated by Gareth Evan Golrad. Notre Dame: University of Notre Dame Press, 2009.

———. "Saint Louis et la prière." In *Horizons Marins, Itinéraires Spirituels (Ve–XVIIIe Siècles)*, edited by Henry Dubois et al., 85–94. Paris: Publications de la Sorbonne, 1987.

Little, Lester K. "Saint Louis' Involvement with the Friars." *Church History* 33 (1965) 125–48.

Lohfink, Norbert F. *Option for the Poor: The Basic Principle of Liberation Theology in the Light of the Bible*. Translated by Linda M. Maloney. Berkeley, CA: BIBAL, 1987.

Maccono, Ferdinando. *Vita di s. Ferdinando III re di Leone e di Castiglia (1198?–1252)*. Milan: Casa Editrice S. Lega Eucaristica, 1924. http://books.google.com/books?id=5XYsAAAAIAAJ.

Marie, Antoine. "April 8, 2008, Eastertide." Abbey of Saint-Joseph de Clairval. https://www.clairval.com/documents/AN-2008-04-08.pdf.

———. "August 6, 2014, Feast of Transfiguration of Our Lord." Abbey of Saint-Joseph de Clairval. http://www.clairval.com/lettres/en/2014/08/06/2060814.htm.

Marshall, Henrietta Elizabeth. "Malcolm Canmore—How Saint Margaret Came to Scotland." Heritage History. https://www.heritage-history.com/index.php?c=read&author=marshall&book=scotland&story=margaret.

Martin, Emmie and Tanza Loudenback. "The 20 Most Generous People in the World." *Independent*, Dec. 2, 2015. https://www.independent.co.uk/news/people/the-20-most-generous-people-in-the-world-a6757046.html.

Martin, Louis and Zélie Martin. *A Call to a Deeper Love: The Family Correspondence of the Parents of St. Therese of the Child Jesus, 1863–1885*. Translated by Ann Connors Hess, edited by Frances Renda. New York: St. Pauls, 2011.

McGuckin, J. A. "The Vine and the Elm Tree: The Patristic Interpretation of Jesus' Teachings on Wealth." In *The Church and Wealth*, edited by W. J. Sheils and Diana Wood, 1–14. Oxford: Basil Blackwell, 1987.

McRoberts, David. *St. Margaret Queen of Scotland*. EWTN. https://www.ewtn.com/catholicism/library/st-margaret-queen-of-scotland-5866.

Menocal, María Rosa. *The Ornament of the World: How Muslims, Jews, and Christians Created a Culture of Tolerance in Medieval Spain*. Boston: Little, Brown, 2002.

Menzies, Lucy. *St. Margaret: Queen of Scotland*. Somerset, UK: Llanerch, 1992.

Mercier, Charles. "Frédéric Ozanam et la misère." In *Frédéric Ozanam: Prophète de la miséricorde*, edited by Rémi Caucanas. Marseille: Chemins de Dialogue, 2015.

Molinari, Paolo, ed. *Summarium super miracolo tributo intercessioni beatae Victoriae Rasoamanarivo, mulieris laicae*. Vatican: Congregatio de Causis Sanctorum, 2007.

Molla, Pietro and Elio Guerriero. *Saint Gianna Molla: Wife, Mother, Doctor*. Translated by James G. Colbert. San Francisco: Ignatius, 2004.

Mousin, Craig B. "Frédéric Ozanam—Beneficent Deserter: Mediating the Chasm of Income Inequality through Liberty, Equality, and Fraternity." *Vincentian Heritage Journal* 30 (2010) 58–80.

Bibliography

Nagy, Kázmér. *St. Margaret of Scotland and Hungary*. Glasgow: John S. Burns, 1973.

Nash, Penelope. *Empress Adelheid and Countess Matilda: Medieval Female Leadership and the Foundation of European Society*. New York: Palgrave Macmillan, 2017.

Odilo of Cluny. *The Epitaph of Adelheid*. In *Queenship and Sanctity: The Lives of Mathilda and the Epitaph of Adelheid*. Translated by Sean Gilsdorf, 128–143. Washington, DC: Catholic University of America Press, 2004.

Office of the Postulator General of the Discalced Carmelites. "Biographical Profile of the Venerable Servants of God: Louis Martin (August 22, 1823—July 29, 1894) and Zélie Martin (December 23, 1831—August 28, 1877)." Translated by Susan Ehler. Solemn Beatification, Basilica of Lisieux, Oct. 19, 2008. http://static1.squarespace.com/static/52709303e4b08363c17ac8fd/t/54dc0127e4b01b81e4da47f3/1423704359484/biographical+profile+of+the+venerable+servants+of+god.pdf.

O'Meara, Kathleen. *Frédéric Ozanam, Professor at the Sorbonne: His Life and Works*. Edinburgh: Edmonston & Douglas, 1876.

O'Neel, Brian. *Thirty-Nine New Saints You Should Know*. Woodrige, IL: Servant, 2010.

Ozanam, Frédéric. *Frédéric Ozanam: A Life in Letters*. Translated and edited by Joseph I. Dirvin. St. Louis: Society of St. Vincent de Paul, 1986.

Papàsogli, Giorgio. *Quesi borghesi . . . I beati Luigi e Maria Beltrame Quattrocchi*. Siena: Edizioni Cantagalli, 2001.

Parisse, Michel. "Adélaïde de Bourgogne, Rein d'Italie et de Germanie, Impératrice (931–999)." In *Adélaïde de Bourgogne: Genèse et représentations d'une sainteté impériale*, edited by Patrick Corget et al., 11–26. Dijon: Editions Universitaires de Dijon, 2002.

Pastoral Centre. "Life of St. Gianna Beretta Molla." https://www.pastoralcentre.pl/index.php/st-gianna-beretta-molla/.

Pasquale, Luca. *Luigi e Maria Beltrame Quattrocchi: Dove vi porta l'amore*. Gorle, IT: Editrice Velar, 2011.

Pedretti, Carolo. *Sant' Omobono: Profeta della carita*. Cremona, IT: Industria Grafica Editoriale Pizzorni, 1969.

Pelucchi, Giuliana. *Saint Gianna Beretta Molla: A Woman's Life, 1922–1962*. Translated by Paul Duggan. Boston: Pauline, 2002.

Pettinati, Guido. "Beata Delfina di Signe: Contessa di Ariano." *Santi, Beati e Testimoni*, last updated Oct. 14, 2008. http://www.santiebeati.it/dettaglio/90451.

Philanthropy Roundtable. "Who Gives Most to Charity?" 2018. https://www.philanthropyroundtable.org/almanac/statistics/who-gives.

Piat, Stéphane Joseph. *The Story of a Family: The Home of the Little Flower*. Translated by A Benedictine of Stanbrook Abbey. New York: P. J. Kenedy & Sons, 1947.

Ramahery, J. L. C. *L'ange visible de l'église naissance a Madagascar: Nouvelle biographie de Victoire Rasoamanarivo*. N.p.: n.p., 1993.

Razafy-Andriamihaingo, Jean-Pierre. "Victoire Rasoamanarivo, notre sainte nationale—3ème partie—ses actes heroïques." *Labodiplo*, Jan. 11, 2016. https://labodiplo.wordpress.com/2016/01/11/victoire-rasoamanarivo-notre-sainte-nationale-3eme-partie-ses-actes-heroiques/.

Renda, Frances. Introduction to *A Call to a Deeper Love: The Family Correspondence of the Parents of St. Thérèse of the Child Jesus, 1863—1885*, by Zélie and Louis Martin, xxi–xxix. Translated by Ann Connors Hess, edited by Frances Renda. New York: St. Pauls, 2011.

Bibliography

Ricci, Adelaide. "'Nel catalogo dei santi': Riflessioni sulla santità di Omobono." In *Strenna dell'ADAFA per l'anno 2011*, 77–93. Cremona, IT: ADAFA, 2012. https://www.adafa.it/wp-content/uploads/2018/10/strenna-2011.pdf.

———. "OMOBONO da Cremona." In *Dizionario Biografico degli Italiani*. Vol. 79. 2013. http://www.treccani.it/enciclopedia/omobono-da-cremona_(Dizionario-Biografico)/.

Richard, Jean. *St. Louis: Crusader King of France*. Translated by Jean Birrell. Cambridge: Cambridge University Press, 1992.

Roosevelt, Theodore. *Theodore Roosevelt: An Autobiography*. New York: Macmillan, 1913.

———. "To Frederick Scott Oliver, August 9, 1906." In *The Letters of Theodore Roosevelt*, edited by Elting Morison and John Blum, 6:349–52. Cambridge: Harvard University Press, 1951–54.

Ruddy, Daniel. *Theodore Roosevelt's History of the United States*. New York: HarperCollins, 2010.

Rybolt, John E. "The Virtuous Personality of Blessed Frederick Ozanam." In *Vincentian Heritage Journal* 17.1 (1996) 35–44.

Savior.org. "Blessed Luigi Beltrame Quattrocchi and Blessed Maria Corsini: 1880–1951, 1884–1965." https://www.savior.org/saints/blessed-luigi-beltrame-quattrocchi-blessed-maria-corsini/.

Schneider Berrenberg, Rüdiger. *Adelheid*. Bonn Am Rhein: Berrenberg, 1999.

Scott, M. M. Maxwell. "Frédéric Ozanam." *Dublin Review* 154.308–9 (1914) 33–50.

Sheehan, Arthur, and Elizabeth Odell. *Pierre Toussaint: A Citizen of Old New York*. New York: P. J. Kenedy & Sons, 1955.

Sickinger, Raymond L. *Antoine Frédéric Ozanam*. Notre Dame: University of Notre Dame Press, 2017.

Simon-Perret, François. *Victoire Rasoamanarivo: Une Chrétienne dans toute sa stature de laïque*. Voreppe, France: Atelier Claire Joie, 1995.

Sivery, Gérard. *L'économie du royaume de France au siecle de Saint Louis*. Lille: Presses Universitaires de Lille, 1984.

Slattery, Kevin. *Blessed Frederic Ozanam: A Life in Outline*. Melbourne: St Vincent de Paul Society, Victoria, 2003.

Spadaro, Antonio. "The Prosperity Gospel: Dangerous and Different." *La Civiltà Cattolica*, July 18, 2018. https://www.laciviltacattolica.com/the-prosperity-gospel-dangerous-and-different/.

Tarry, Ellen. *Pierre Toussaint: Apostle of Old New York*. 2nd ed. Boston: Pauline, 1998.

Theoharis, Liz. *Always with Us? What Jesus Really Said about the Poor*. Grand Rapids: Eerdmans, 2017.

Thierry, Augustin. *Tales of the Early Franks: Episodes from Merovingian History*. Translated by M. F. O. Jenkins. Tuscaloosa, AL: University of Alabama Press, 1977.

Turgot. *The Dunfermline Vita*. Translated by Catherine Keene. In *Saint Margaret: Queen of the Scots: A Life in Perspective*, by Catherine Keene, 138–221. New York: Palgrave Macmillan, 2013.

———. *Vita Margaretae*. In *Ancient Lives of Scottish Saints*, translated by W. M. Metcalfe, 295–321. Paisley, UK: Alexander Gardner, 1895.

Unienville, Raymond d'. "Victoire Rasoamanarivo, la bienheureuse notre soeur malgache." *L'Express*, Sept. 13, 2004. https://lexpress.mu/s/article/victoire-rasoamanarivo-la-bienheureuse-notre-soeur-malgache.

Bibliography

———. "Victoire Rasoamanarivo: la Bienheureuse (suite et fin)." *L'Express*, Oct. 18, 2024. https://lexpress.mu/article/victoire-rasoamanarivo-la-bienheureuse-suite-et-fin.

Vauchez, André. *The Laity in the Middle Ages: Religious Beliefs and Devotional Practices*. Translated by Margery J. Schneider. Notre Dame: University of Notre Dame Press, 1993.

———. *Omobono di Cremona (1197): Laico e santo; Profilo storico*. Cremona: Nuova editrice cremonese, 2001.

———. "Saint Homebon († 1197), patron des marchands et des artisans drapiers à la fin du Moyen Âge et à l'époque moderne." In *Chemins d'outre-mer*, edited by Damien Coulon, 839–46. Paris: Éditions de la Sorbonne, 2004. https://doi.org/10.4000/books.psorbonne.4017.

———. *Sainthood in the Later Middle Ages*. Translated by Jean Birrell. New York: Cambridge University Press, 1997.

———. "Le 'trafiquant céleste': Saint Homebon de Crémone (+1197); Marchand et 'père des pauvres.'" In *Horizons marins, itinéraires spirituels (V^e–XVIIIe siècles)*, edited by Henry Dubois et al., 1:115–22. Histoire ancienne et médiévale 20. Paris: Publications de la Sorbonne, 1987.

Vanzan, Piersandro. "Maria e Luigi Beltrame Quattrocchi: Storia di un amore cristiano." *La Civiltà Cattolica* 158.3771–72 (Aug. 4, 2007) 246–56.

Vatican News. "Gianna Beretta Molla (1922–1962)." May 16, 2004. http://www.vatican.va/news_services/liturgy/saints/ns_lit_doc_20040516_beretta-molla_en.html.

———. "Luigi Beltrame Quattrocchi (1880–1951) e Maria Corsini vedova Beltrame Quattrocchi (1884–1965)." Oct. 10, 2001. http://www.vatican.va/news_services/liturgy/documents/ns_lit_doc_20011021_quattrocchi_it.html.

VincentWiki. "Systemic Change: Seeds of Change." Famvin. https://www.famvin.org/wiki/Systemic_Change:_Seeds_of_Change.

Wallace, Susan Helen, and Patricia Edward Jablonski. *Saint Gianna Beretta Molla: The Gift of Life*. Boston: Pauline, 2012.

Ward, Kate. *Wealth, Virtue and Moral Luck: Christian Ethics in an Age of Inequality*. Washington, DC: Georgetown University Press, 2021.

Wikipedia. "Adélaïde de Bourgogne." Last updated Dec. 12, 2024. https://fr.wikipedia.org/wiki/Ad%C3%A9la%C3%AFde_de_Bourgogne#Biographie.

———. "Adelaide di Borgogna (Imperatrice)." Last updated Jan. 2, 2025. https://it.wikipedia.org/wiki/Adelaide_di_Borgogna_(imperatrice).

———. "Adelaide of Italy." Last updated Jan. 5, 2025. https://en.wikipedia.org/wiki/Adelaide_of_Italy.

———. "Delphine de Sabran." Last updated Feb. 22, 2024. https://fr.wikipedia.org/wiki/Delphine_de_Sabran.

———. "Elzéar de Sabron." Last updated June 26, 2024. https://fr.wikipedia.org/wiki/Elz%C3%A9ar_de_Sabran.

———. "Ferdinand III of Castile." Last updated Jan. 13, 2025. https://en.wikipedia.org/wiki/Ferdinand_III_of_Castile.

———. "Frédéric Ozanam." Last updated Jan. 13, 2025. https://en.wikipedia.org/wiki/Fr%C3%A9d%C3%A9ric_Ozanam.

———. "Gianna Beretta Molla." Last updated Nov. 6, 2024. https://en.wikipedia.org/wiki/Gianna_Beretta_Molla.

———. "Guntram." Last updated Jan. 20, 2025. https://en.wikipedia.org/wiki/Guntram.

Bibliography

———. "Guntram I." Last updated Sept. 18, 2024. https://de.wikipedia.org/wiki/Guntram_I.

———. "Homobon de Crémone." Last updated July 22, 2024. https://fr.wikipedia.org/wiki/Homobon_de_Cr%C3%A9mone.

———. "Joan, Countess of Ponthieu." Last updated Dec. 1, 2024. https://en.wikipedia.org/wiki/Joan,_Countess_of_Ponthieu.

———. "List of Philanthropists." Last updated Jan. 16, 2025. https://en.wikipedia.org/wiki/List_of_philanthropists.

———. "Louis IX." Last updated Jan. 22, 2025. https://fr.wikipedia.org/wiki/Louis_IX.

———. "Louis IX of France." Last updated Jan. 15, 2025. https://en.wikipedia.org/wiki/Louis_IX_of_France.

———. "Louis Martin and Marie-Azélie Guérin." Last updated Dec. 30, 2024. https://en.wikipedia.org/wiki/Louis_Martin_and_Marie-Azélie_Guérin.

———. "Ludwig IX. (Frankreich)." Last updated Dec. 7, 2024. https://de.wikipedia.org/wiki/Ludwig_IX._(Frankreich).

———. "Omobono Tucenghi." Last updated Dec. 10, 2024. https://it.wikipedia.org/wiki/Omobono_Tucenghi.

———. "Saint Homobonus." Last updated Jan. 22, 2025. https://en.wikipedia.org/wiki/Saint_Homobonus.

———. "Saint Margaret of Scotland." Last updated Dec. 22, 2024. https://en.wikipedia.org/wiki/Saint_Margaret_of_Scotland.

Wilson, A. J. *St. Margaret: Queen of Scotland.* 2nd ed. Edinburgh: John Donald, 2001.

Wood, Ian. *The Merovingian Kingdoms, 450–751.* London: Longman, 1994.

Wust, Louis and Majorie Wust. *Louis Martin: An Ideal Father.* Derby, NY: Daughters of St. Paul, 1953.

Zeno.org. "Homobonus, S." *Vollständiges Heiligen-Lexikon.* http://www.zeno.org/nid/20002984474.

Ziegler, J. J. "History Awaits in Canonization of Married Couple." *OSV Newsweekly*, Apr. 22, 2015. https://aliveinchrist.osv.com/parish/article/history_awaits_in_canonization_of_married_couple.

www.ingramcontent.com/pod-product-compliance
Lightning Source LLC
Chambersburg PA
CBHW050822160426
43192CB00010B/1863